UNLOCK YOUR LEADERSHIP SKILLS: 30-DAY LEADERSHIP COURSE FOR BEGINNERS, NEW BUSINESS LEADERS, AND MANAGERS IN THE WORKPLACE

INSPIRE, EMPOWER, AND INFLUENCE TEAMS

OLALEKAN ASIPA

TABLE OF CONTENTS

Introduction	vii
1. WHAT IS LEADERSHIP?	1
Defining Leadership	2
Transformational Leadership	5
Characteristics of Successful Leaders	9
Visionary Leaders	12
Reflection Time	13
2. UNDERSTANDING LEADERSHIP	16
Understanding Leadership	17
Qualities of a Leader	18
Leadership Styles	21
Choosing Your Leadership Style	28
Leadership Training	29
Leadership for Diverse Groups	30
Top Ten Leadership Principles	37
Reflection Time	38
3. LEADERSHIP SKILLS FOR THE WORKPLACE	40
Essential Leadership Skills	41
How to Showcase Your Skills	45
Improve Your Leadership Skills	48
Top Ten Tips for Becoming a Leader	50
Reflection Time	52
4. DEALING WITH THE OUT-GROUP	54
Why Do Out-Groups Exist?	55
Out-Groups Do Have Impact	57
Strategies for Responding to the Out-Group	58
When the Out-Group Stays Out	58
Don't Forget an Out-Group	60

Microaggressions: How to Avoid Them	62
Common Pitfalls Leaders Make	64
Trends for Inclusion	65
Reflection Time	66
5. NEGOTIATION IN THE WORKPLACE	**68**
What is Negotiation?	68
Stages of Negotiation	71
Ways to Approach Conflict	74
Top Ten Negotiation Skills	77
How to Protect Yourself During a Negotiation	78
Reflection Time	80
6. TEAM MANAGEMENT	**82**
Motivation is Key	84
Management Styles: Pros and Cons	89
Micromanagement versus Macromanagement	94
Reflection Time	96
7. EMOTIONAL INTELLIGENCE	**98**
What is Emotional Intelligence?	99
Why is Emotional Intelligence Important?	103
EQ Matters More Than IQ	104
Building Emotional Intelligence	105
How to Use Your Emotional Intelligence	108
Improving Your Emotional Intelligence	108
Potential Pitfalls	110
Reflection Time	111
8. INFLUENTIAL LEADERS OF THE WORLD	**113**
Bill Gates	114
Jack Welsh	116
Steve Jobs	119
Warren Buffett	123
Reflection Time	126
Conclusion	127
References	133

© Copyright 2022 - All rights reserved.

The content contained within this book may not be reproduced, duplicated or transmitted without direct written permission from the author or the publisher.

Under no circumstances will any blame or legal responsibility be held against the publisher, or author, for any damages, reparation, or monetary loss due to the information contained within this book, either directly or indirectly.

Legal Notice:

This book is copyright protected. It is only for personal use. You cannot amend, distribute, sell, use, quote or paraphrase any part, or the content within this book, without the consent of the author or publisher.

Disclaimer Notice:

Please note the information contained within this document is for educational and entertainment purposes only. All effort has been executed to present accurate, up to date, reliable, complete information. No warranties of any kind are declared or implied. Readers acknowledge that the author is not engaged in the rendering of legal, financial, medical or professional advice. The content within this book has been derived from various sources. Please consult a licensed professional before attempting any techniques outlined in this book.

By reading this document, the reader agrees that under no circumstances is the author responsible for any losses, direct or indirect, that are incurred as a result of the use of the information contained within this document, including, but not limited to, errors, omissions, or inaccuracies.

 Created with Vellum

GIFT

Just For You!

A FREE GIFT TO OUR READERS

A – Z of leadership which contain popular leadership quotes by influential leaders! Visit this link below or scan QR Code:

https://oainc.activehosted.com/f/5

INTRODUCTION
LEADERSHIP IS INFLUENCE. –JOHN C. MAXWELL

Are you contemplating a career change? Do you want more influence at your workplace? Do you ever stop and wonder: What is good leadership? Maybe you feel unsure of yourself and fear stepping into a leadership position at work. Either way, you don't have to have an elaborate title to become a leader. Anyone can lead. You just need to learn how and choose to do it.

Leaders are the movers and shakers of the world. They can mobilize others to action. Given the current world climate, leaders are needed now more than ever. In an ever-changing world, leadership is the one thing that remains constant. Luckily for us, leadership is not some fad that will disappear next week. Now is the time for you to rise in the ranks of leadership. Communities need leaders like you. However, it's not easy to pin down the exact definition of outstanding leadership. That's why I needed to write this book.

At the end of the 30-day course, you should be able to

Introduction

create an action plan and self-assess your current leadership profile. Leadership is often viewed as a game. For example, everyone loves to watch a good game of college basketball. A set of predetermined rules guide these organized sports. These rules are accepted universally, and it doesn't matter the level of the playing field. Sometimes, people like to add their local traditions. Adapting the rules keeps things interesting. The same applies to leadership.

Think about all the rules and regulations you encounter in your everyday life and workplace. These principles help identify what is acceptable and unacceptable regarding the type of work and how your managers and supervisors behave. It even comes down to intricate details of your workplace: wages, safety, reporting, etc. Often, these rules and regulations are mandatory. In the workplace, managers and supervisors need to stay on top of knowing how to manage their game. As the game unfolds, it helps influential leaders stand out amongst the crowd when they recognize, master, and apply the rules proactively.

For the ordinary spectator, these games can seem one-dimensional. But, in reality, they are incredibly complex, as are situations in the workplace. Even the subtle nuances can make a significant difference in how people participate. It's so easy to act like you know how to play the game. But when push comes to shove, so many complexities go into playing the leadership game.

I completely understand if you feel the crunch. Embracing your leadership skills can be an emotional roller coaster. The number one complaint I've heard from people in my career is that they feel overwhelmed and don't have

Introduction

the time to lead effectively. These feelings can be 100% valid, but I am also here to tell you—this can be a mindset issue.

It would be best if you navigated things differently than before. You are not alone. It will be essential to figure out a few elements that pertain to your position as a leader: objectives, deadlines, culture, and the personalities of your co-workers and followers. It doesn't matter where you are currently in the game. You can learn new skills. And, if you're already a skilled leader, you can become a better leader by working on your known weaknesses.

Leadership is a journey. In the next 30 days, I hope you learn about more game rules, recognize the skills you already possess, and practice them effectively. The more you learn, the better leader you will become. If you understand them all, people will want to follow you. Just know that Rome was not built in a day. It will take time and likely longer than 30 days. This text provides concrete ways to create habits that will transform your leadership skills. This book is for individuals ready to take their game to the next level.

This journey will allow you to see leadership differently and build more plays for your playbook. These skills will help you see leadership in others and understand what it takes to be a transformational leader. It's also essential to recognize that leadership constantly fluxes in re-evaluation. Therefore, you'll need to reflect upon your leadership strengths and traits. It's a forever-changing spectrum that will need to change over time as situations change and you grow as an individual.

It feels like the writing of a book has been a lifetime in the making throughout my career. Looking back on my life, I have always enjoyed sharing the leadership information with others that will be presented on the following pages. Even though I wrote the book, many people have guided me over the years. I wish I could acknowledge them all. As an engineer, I have several years of experience in leadership, especially in managing teams. I believe the world deserves competent, understanding, and emotionally intelligent leaders. I want to help you understand what it takes to become a respected individual in business and the workplace. Being a force for change, I enjoy helping people rise to their potential. Therefore, I have decided to write this book to enlighten readers about leadership and influence others to become great leaders.

Overview of the Book

This book intends to serve as a practice-oriented book. You'll find this text offers a user-friendly writing style that's appropriate for an introduction to leadership. Each chapter is written in short sections. You can start at the beginning and read it the whole way through. Or, you can look at the table of contents and find a section that interests you. Either way, there are many meaningful ideas to add to your current leadership skill set:

- Leadership & Transformational Leadership
- Understanding Leadership
- Leadership Skills for the Workplace
- Examples of Influential Leaders
- Negotiation in the Workplace
- Team Management

- Emotional Intelligence

It is well-suited for programs in leadership studies and courses to supplement their existing curriculum and continuing education for those in the workforce. As I share these ground rules, I hope the information presented allows you to lead with a purpose. This text will provide a general roadmap and practical recommendations you should take to become a successful leader. It will bring confidence and effectiveness to your leadership style if you are willing to work.

Are you ready to lead? Keep reading.

1
WHAT IS LEADERSHIP?

Leadership and learning are indispensable to each other. –John F. Kennedy

What is leadership? It's a straightforward question, yet many people struggle to answer it. There is this belief in the world that it takes someone who has a title or is charismatic. The truth is that anyone can be a leader. It's not some innate trait that you are born with. It's an accumulation of skills learned and developed over time. Yet, defining leadership seems to have vexed even the smartest of individuals.

Let us start with what leadership is not...

It is not seniority.

It is not a person's title.

It is not about a person's personal attributes.

It is not management.

It is not power or authority.

So, what is leadership?

Answering this question can get a little overwhelming. You might want to explore eleven different leadership styles on your own time: servant, authentic, democratic, visionary, charismatic, coaching, affiliative, empathetic, pacesetting, commanding, and situational. You might find that you ascribe to several leadership styles—or, at the very least, find value in certain pieces of each leadership style. There is no one-size-fits-all leadership style. You have to find what works for you.

First, you must get to know yourself. There are a variety of personality and self-assessments that exist in the world. For example, Gallup's StrengthsFinder or a Leadership 360 assessment can help you know where you stand and the types of individuals you might want to surround yourself with to help transform an organization.

You will need to answer this fundamental question: What is my leadership style?

This journey will take honesty on your part and your ability to accept constructive feedback from others. It will also take grit and hard work to recognize your strengths and weaknesses and grow as an individual and leader.

Are you ready?

Defining Leadership

It depends on who you talk with. Definitions will vary. Leadership can mean different things to different people around the world. It also depends on the various situations people can experience. At its core, leadership is the process of social influence. This influence maximizes the efforts of those you work with and help them achieve a goal. It seems simple, right? It should be. Outstanding leadership can be a difficult thing to understand.

John C. Maxwell developed the five myths about leadership in his book The 21 Irrefutable Laws of Leadership. Here is what I have come to understand about those five myths.

1. The Management Myth

How many people have you talked to that claim leadership and being in an administrative position go hand-in-hand? Leadership is not having a managerial role. It's about influencing people. All management does is worry about a company's systems and processes, not about the people. According to Maxwell, the best test to see if a person can lead is to ask them to make a positive change. Having the ability to manage others will inevitably require influence.

Effective leadership is the ability to inspire others, but it's also how you choose to lead your life as an individual. You do not have to have a title to be a leader. You need a set of skills that anyone can master. Leading also takes a certain level of empathy and connection to those you are trying to lead.

2. The Entrepreneur Myth

I have heard this myth perpetuated in the workplace. Just because someone is an entrepreneur doesn't mean they are a natural-born leader. Entrepreneurs can often see opportunities that no one else does and go after them. Their motive for doing so is fueled by innovation or profit. These fast thinkers are not always good at dealing with people. Therefore, CEOs tend to find managers who can deal with the people portion. This goes back to the definition of effective leadership. Leadership equals influence.

3. The Knowledge Myth

Say it with me, power is not leadership—just the same as knowledge is not leadership, either. An individual can be remarkably brilliant and still lack the capacity to lead others. Amount of education, standardized test scores, and a high IQ do not equal being a great leader.

4. The Pioneer Myth

If someone is the first to do something, it doesn't automatically qualify them to be a leader. A true leader recognizes those who come along beside them, those who came first, and those coming in behind them. Likewise, an individual might be a trendsetter but that doesn't mean they are a leader.

5. The Position Myth

People think that leadership is based on position and titles. It's not. It's the influence of the person that matters. If a CEO is asked to leave their position and they have a large level of influence, some followers may also leave the company out of principle.

The 30-day journey you are about to embark upon will help you define what leadership looks like to you and build plays for your playbook to use in the future. Once you've determined your leadership style, your game will be even more robust. What you learn on this journey should be practical and repeatable.

Once you figure out all the factors that go into the game, you will emerge as a leader. Zig Ziglar once said, "It is true that integrity alone won't make you a leader, but without integrity you will never be one" (AZ Quotes, n.d.). Therefore, Maxwell's five myths should play an integral part in your playbook.

It's important to remember that leaders help themselves

and others. They encourage people to do ethical things. Leaders set the tone to achieve goals. They must paint an inspiring vision that others will not want to miss out on being a part of. That's why this next section is vital. The transformational leadership model proposed by James MacGregor Burns and developed by Bernard M. Bass paints a picture of how to become a visionary thinker to bring change to your organization.

Transformational Leadership

James MacGregor Burns came up with the idea of transformational leadership in 1978.

"According to the idea of transformational leadership, an effective leader is a person who does the following: creates an inspiring vision of the future; motivates and inspires people to engage with that vision; manages the delivery of the vision; and, coaches and builds a team, so that it is more effective at achieving the vision" (Mind Tools Content Team, 2009).

We must explore all four elements of transformational leadership to build new plays for your playbook. This type of leadership is proactive. If you're a problem solver that's not satisfied with the status quo, this is for you.

A prime example of a transformation leader would be Steve Jobs. He was a world-renowned transformational leader. Jobs is practically a household name since Apple is everywhere. It has been said by those who worked for Jobs that he was constantly encouraging people to push the envelope. He was an innovative thinker. To think, it all started in his garage. Transformational leadership allowed Jobs to give his employees the creative platform to bring about change. He had success with this type of leadership because his organizational structure was able to see growth and improve the lives of his staff while also creating products that have changed the world as we know it today. Jobs was a transformational leader, but he was also a visionary leader.

If a leader creates an inspiring vision for the future, it allows the leader to provide a direction. A vision is an accurate, realistic, and convincing depiction of what individuals want for the future. You can tell your vision is solid if people can fully understand and embrace the idea. You need to paint a vivid picture of the future and tell compelling stories that back up your vision.

To create this vision, you may consider using the following tools to analyze your current workplace.

- Strength Weakness Opportunity Threat (SWOT) Analysis
- Political, Economic, Social, and Technological (PEST) Analysis
- Unique Selling Proposition (USP) Analysis
- Core Competence Analysis
- Porter's Five Forces Template
- The template includes the following forces: supplier power, buyer power, rivalry among existing competitors, the threat of substitute products or services, and threat of new entrants.

These analysis structures provide proof of an organization's strengths that can be used to develop strategies to help the organization thrive in the marketplace. In addition, the data gathered can be used to support research on how your competitors will respond and how to bring change to your workplace.

A vision helps others become motivated because they understand where the organization is going. Having a shared vision will help people change how they see their work. It creates value. You may already have a vision statement for your organization under the guise of a mission statement. Be sure not to let it just be something that hangs on the wall. Embody that vision. It's important to understand that vision is not a value. "Don't mistake an esoteric list of values teamwork, excellence, and the like for vision" (Bradberry & Greaves, 2012, p. 26).

Once you've painted this picture, it will help you motivate and inspire the people that work with you. If they buy into the concept, it will help you deliver it. Your enthusiasm for the change needs to shine through for all to see. Joy is infectious. The tricky thing will be to keep that momentum going even through the rough times. You might want to consider using some reward as people succeed, whether intrinsic or extrinsic.

How do you know you have a clear vision? Consider the following questions presented by Bradberry and Greaves (2012, p. 27-28) to see if your vision is complete:

- Is the bigger picture easy for others to see?
- Does the concept stimulate their interest and get their juices flowing?
- Does my vision get people moving spontaneously?
- Is my idea realistic?

- Is my vision so clear that people can spread the word?
- Would everyone continue to pursue this vision even in my absence?

If you answered yes to all of these questions, you can begin developing a plan to lead your team to success. You must have credibility in this process. People need to know they can trust you. They must trust that you are a resident expert to bring this idea to fruition. Managing the delivery of the vision is the only part that involves management in transformational leadership. You must trust that people will work for you to make the dream happen. This process must be properly managed. You might take the lead yourself or delegate tasks to your organization's managers.

Transformational leadership includes coaching and building a team to achieve your vision. Remember your playbook? Your team needs to have the skills to do their job. You can do this by promptly giving valuable feedback. Feedback needs to happen frequently, not just annually. People don't know if they're doing something incorrectly if they're not told in a constructive manner. The feedback you give should improve performance for the individual and the team if you do it professionally. Helping others develop their skills is the real test of an influential leader. If building people up intrigues you, you should also investigate servant leadership.

Characteristics of Successful Leaders

Bass later further developed transformational leadership in 1978 to include characteristics of a transformational leader.

Transformational leadership characteristics encompass the following:

- being a model of integrity and fairness
- authenticity
- open communication with others
- setting clear and concise goals
- have high expectations for themselves and others
- encouraging others to take ownership of tasks
- providing support and recognition to those who help the organization succeed
- stirring the emotions of people in a positive way
- getting people to look beyond themselves
- inspiring people to reach for the impossible
- focusing on coaching and mentoring
- delegating decision-making
- creating a supportive work environment and culture with clear values and high standards of ethics and morals

So, what can you be doing in the meantime?

Here are some qualities you can focus on to become a better leader:

- Work on building your confidence.
- Learn how to focus on your goals.
- Create a vision for your own life and the world.

- Be resilient.
- Be honest.
- Try to be positive and empower others. (This might take some work!)
- Learn how to make difficult decisions.
- Inspire others.
- Be an effective communicator.
- Be accountable for your actions.
- Show empathy to others.
- Have humility. (It's not a weakness.)
- Be creative.
- Make connections with everyone you meet.

There will always be pros and cons to each leadership type. Therefore, you must evaluate them carefully before deciding that transformational leadership is right for you. This list, of course, is not exclusive, and there may be more pros and cons that you add to the list yourself.

Pros

- competency to convey new ideas to others
- knows the difference between their long-term goals and short-term vision
- promotes collaboration within the organization
- focuses on relationship building to establish trust
- gives everyone an equal chance to perform in creative and innovative ways
- employees feel seen and valued

Cons

- inadequate leadership style for bureaucratic organizations
- leaves opportunities open for employees to fail and not get things done
- distracts people from the immediate needs of the organization
- poor fit for those who need more guidance and supervision

How does one become a transformational leader? Bass' characteristics can give you some realistic goals to focus on for the next 30 days and beyond. It involves four steps.

1. Spend some time creating an inspiring vision and culture for your workplace.
2. Once you have a vision in mind, work to motivate people to buy into it.
3. Create a team that helps you deliver the vision and decide how you will manage all of it.
4. This will only happen if you build relationships based on trust with people.

Easy, right? Well, maybe not so much.

It can seem like a daunting task if you've never done this. Go back to your organization's mission and vision statements. What does the company stand for? Have you taken the time to analyze your work environment? If not, use Mullin's Seven Domains Model. Have you developed a strategy before? The Lafley and Martin's Five-Step Strategy Model can guide you to build your plan.

At the end of this chapter, you'll have space to contemplate whether or not you are a transformational leader. I thought I would mention an incredible resource that will help you develop your playbook even further. Hugh Blane offers a Transformational Leadership Assessment that will help you rate yourself. Assessments can be a quick gut check to see where your current mindset is. I highly recommend buying the 7 Principles of Transformational Leadership: Create a Mindset of Passion, Innovation, and Growth by Hugh Blane to take the assessment.

Visionary Leaders

The term visionary leader sounds unattainable. However, the critical thing to remember is that this visionary leadership does not have to be world-changing. Anyone can be a visionary leader. You might even be one and not be aware of it. A visionary leader is an individual who sees the potential for how the world should be and knows how to get there (Lucas, 2021).

Visionary leaders are risk-takers and crave change. Sometimes, change means taking risks. Do not be afraid to embrace change. Innovative leaders can listen. The people that work for you need to know they will be heard. The next time you have a conversation, take some time to assess whether you were participating in active listening or not.

There are a variety of traits associated with being a visionary leader. Typically, people find them to be inspirational. They have that uncanny ability to convey their passion to others. They can tap into the hidden potential of everyone. Of course, they need to be strategic. Without a plan, nothing would get done. They also don't allow obstacles to get in the way. Visionary leaders are charismatic. Charisma helps them to engage others in the process. Since they are hard workers, they are also persistent. They do the best they can, but they also help others achieve greatness. Finally, visionary leaders must be open-minded. They are accepting of new ideas and can be flexible.

Some might even consider Elon Musk to be a visionary leader. Musk also uses transformational leadership to achieve. It's no secret: He is bold and persistent. He also did not become successful all on his own. Musk relies on teams of engineers, designers, and marketers to fulfill his vision. It may seem like he has some lofty goals in mind, but he's a strategic thinker and not afraid of taking small steps to get to where he wants to be. And, just like you, he had to learn leadership skills by doing the work and sometimes failing.

John F. Kennedy once said, "Leadership and learning are indispensable to each other" (Daum, 2016). Never shy away from learning. Acting like you know everything is dangerous for any leader to do. Learning new things is never out for the pro. Challenge yourself and learn something new. Developing leadership skills is essential to anyone's career development. How will you improve your leadership skills? What actions will you take to be an influence?

Reflection Time

Follow effective action with quiet reflection. From the quiet reflection will come even more effective action. –Peter Drucker

Time to reflect upon your current practice. Reflective

practices for transformational leaders allow you to see your processes, feelings, and how you think. Be honest with yourself as you spend time reflecting. It's vital to examine your mindset periodically. Reflection helps you break bad habits and improve your skills as a leader. Find a quiet space and take the time to answer the following questions. It might be helpful to keep a journal during this process to track your growth.

1. What have you learned about yourself so far in this process?
2. What have you learned about leadership that you did not know before?
3. Are there things you learned about your workplace that you did not notice before?
4. Are you seeing how you treat other people and yourself?
5. Do you practice self-care?
6. What is your vision for the future?
7. Are there habits you need to break to fulfill the dream?

As you take the time to ponder the answer to these questions, make a list of the technical skills and soft skills you already possess. Technical skills pertain to your area of knowledge and expertise—skills in technology, analysis, engineering, math, the arts, science, etc. While some believe that knowledge is power, you should also develop your soft skills. These are the character traits and interpersonal skills that help you develop relationships with other people. Later in the book, I will touch upon these skills, especially emotional intelligence. Without soft skills, your likelihood of having success as a leader is minimal.

2
UNDERSTANDING LEADERSHIP

'He who thinks he leads, but has no followers, is only taking a walk' – If you can't influence others, they won't follow you. –
John C. Maxwell

Many people have tried to define leadership to help others fully understand leadership and the various styles of leadership. Unfortunately, there have also been people who have failed because their primary focus was on popularity, power, or wisdom, which is not the core of leadership. It can be dangerous if one only focuses on being in charge instead of focusing on others. In Chapter Two, you'll take a deep dive into really understanding leadership and its styles. Now, it's time to focus on the qualities and principles of leadership, how to train to become a leader, and how to lead diverse groups of people.

Understanding Leadership

Ultimately, leadership can be measured by the amount of influence one possesses. You can see leadership by the number of followers one has. Many factors play into this. Hopefully, by the end of this exercise, you'll realize that title or position has little to no bearing on one's ability to lead. Leadership is an intricate balance of many things. It's more than just being nice to people or understanding them, and there's a fine line between running a business and pushing people around.

In 1961, W.C.H. Prentice wrote an article that rejected the thought that leadership was about power and force or an unique skill set. Under his guise, leadership is often defined as "the accomplishment of a goal through the direction of human assistants" (Harvard Business Review, 2004). A leader should understand how to motivate others and garner their participation to create a sense of purpose amongst the group.

If you wish to advance in your career, leadership skills will be essential to your success. Take the time to get out of your comfort zone and find ways to challenge yourself to grow as an individual and leader in the workplace. The first step in this journey is taking the initiative to do so. Remember, very few of us are born leaders. It takes effort and requires you to do the heavy lifting and volunteer to take on more responsibilities beyond your regular duties. If you have not done this before, it will take time for others to recognize your efforts.

You may not be popular all the time as a leader, but you can have people do things for you out of admiration. Leadership is a tap dance amongst people to focus the attention on the overall goals that accomplish the vision. It also takes a certain level of flexibility on the leader's part to accept the help and ideas that have skills you may not possess yourself. It's about leveraging groups of people to succeed.

So you may be wondering, how do I become a leader? "Leadership development involves identifying and mastering the key skills and characteristics required to become a successful leader" (Yan, 2022). Remember those technical and soft skills mentioned in Chapter One. Now is the time to improve them. In addition, several core leadership skills and qualities should be mastered to become a successful leader.

Leadership is:

- a trait
- an ability
- a skill
- a behavior
- a relationship
- an ongoing process

Qualities of a Leader

Luckily for us, leadership qualities can be learned and improved over time. Across the board, successful leaders demonstrate similar leadership qualities in their personal and professional lives. Therefore, these essential qualities will need practice to strengthen the positive impact on others.

The first thing to work on will be self-awareness and

prioritizing your personal development. Without this, you could have roadblocks in the future. The most effective leaders focus on their emotional intelligence. Maybe you don't know what that is. Don't worry; there is a whole chapter on it. But the short version is that emotional intelligence is the ability to understand, use, and manage your emotions to impact communicating and empathizing with others positively.

You will need to learn how to become more adaptive and be willing to accept feedback from those around you. Be open to change; you never know where it will take you. Focus on the bigger picture. While setting goals and taking responsibility for them, you should also own up to making mistakes. People will appreciate you far more when you become human to them. Be accepting of others. People will make mistakes, and there will be challenges. How you react to the situation will make all the difference.

It will also be essential for you to know the strengths, weaknesses, and potential biases you may have. This could cloud your judgment without acknowledging their existence. You'll also need to set clear boundaries with yourself and others. Burnout is a real thing. Have you ever heard the expression "monkey see, monkey do"? Your followers are watching your every move. If you work on all cylinders all day long, your followers will think they need to do the same thing.

A quality leader focuses on developing others' skill sets. You might need to learn how to delegate tasks and coach or mentor those you work with. As you build a team, look for people who have diverse backgrounds and skills. As a leader, you will need to equip them with the proper tools to do the job or task. Training is an essential part. Richard Branson once said, "Train people well enough so they can leave, but treat them well enough so they don't want to" (Eastwood, 2019). You will also need to show empathy and be assertive at the same. It's not always easy to do. Find balance.

So you might be asking, where is the technical part of leadership? It's true: Strategic thinking, innovation, and action are essential parts of outstanding leadership. "Leaders must consider internal organizational factors, such as product roadmaps and staffing needs, as well as external factors, including government regulations and technology advancement, when making strategic business decisions" (Eastwood, 2019). If you have a college degree, you've already learned much that you need to know about your profession. But how do we grow beyond that knowledge?

Here are a few ideas:

- Have an open mind.
- Take some risks.
- Be enthusiastic.
- Focus on the future.
- Encourage the team to be creative and innovative.
- Set SMART (specific, measurable, attainable, realistic, and timely) goals.

Strong leadership also requires a certain level of ethics. You must use your authority appropriately and with integrity. As you develop this skill, you'll need to be transparent with others, even if you might get some kickback. Own your own mistakes. Take the time to keep your own emotions in check while validating others. Give praise when necessary or lend a helping hand when you see someone struggling.

Effective communication is an element that's essential and yet quickly the most left behind concept in organizations. If you want to be a respected leader, you need to work on your communication skills. Use clear and concise language when explaining tasks, goals, or objectives to those carrying out the charge. It would be best if you communicated the expectation. However, be careful of what you put into writing. Sometimes, people do not understand language nuances, which can come back to bite you. You might have to change your communication style when working with diverse populations.

Possible leadership traits to improve upon are:

- intelligence
- confidence
- charisma
- determination
- sociability
- integrity

Leadership Styles

There are a variety of leadership styles you could potentially ascribe to. A leadership style is a collection of behaviors that leaders possess. It focuses on what leaders do and how they act. Sometimes, it depends on the situation you're in to help you figure out what leadership style works. There can be pros and cons to each type. It also depends on your personality and which kind is right for you. The same goes for the people you work with and their personalities.

In 1939, Kurt Lewin identified the three major types of leadership - authoritarian, democratic, and laissez-faire. These styles are based on the work of Douglas McGregor and his famous book The Human Side of Enterprise (1960). McGregor expanded upon Kurt Lewin's work. In this text, McGregor proposed two theories: Theory X and Theory Y. These theories are based on human behavior and relationships.

Theory X:

- People do not like to work.
- People need to be directed and controlled.
- People do not want responsibility; they want security.

Theory Y:

- People like to work.
- People are self-motivated.
- People accept and seek responsibility.

Let us take some time to examine each leadership style. You may find that you already identify with one without even realizing it.

Authoritarian Leadership Style

The authoritarian leadership style takes on the beliefs laid out by Theory X. These leaders believe their followers need direction. There is a perception that people need to be controlled. Control is often perceived as micromanagement.

Authoritarian leaders love to tell others that they are in charge. In this top-down managerial style, the leaders determine the tasks and procedures. There is not much collaboration in this leadership style; tasks and duties are assigned with very little input from the followers.

Since these leaders love control, they don't encourage communication in the organization. They want to know everything, so all communication goes through them. When giving feedback to others, authoritarian leaders tend to give praise and criticism freely. Unfortunately, their objection is based on their standards rather than being constructive.

Some people would argue that authoritarian leadership is necessary for specific situations. For example, you might have a group of poor-performing people that need more direct supervision, or in times of crisis. It's perceived as a domineering style. Followers can begin to lose interest in the task at hand.

Today, this form of leadership is likely not to be as effective as others. Newer generations are far more independent and do not respond well to control. In addition, there's a new trend in the workplace for individuals to find a job that satisfies them. They are seeking that over collecting a paycheck for little thanks.

Democratic Leadership Style

Democratic leadership style follows closely with McGregor's Theory Y. Democratic leaders encourage others to participate in making decisions and believe that followers can do the work independently. This leadership style helps others reach their goals. Communication flows naturally in this style. It's not top-down like the authoritarian style. Democratic leaders wish to listen to their followers in a supportive way. They also encourage people to talk with one another to solve problems. They believe that people can be self-directed and do not need to hover over them.

This style allows the leader to give guidance and the perception of being friendly. This leadership creates a positive work environment and culture that generates motivation and innovation. In addition, the followers are allowed to participate more freely, increasing their commitment to the organization.

There are several advantages to democratic leadership:

- increased motivation and morale
- increased co-operation within the organization and management
- improved job performance and satisfaction
- reduction of conflict
- reduction of absenteeism and turnover rates

On the flip side, one might argue that this leadership style will take more time to implement. It takes extra commitment on the part of the leader. It could give the perception of trying to herd a group of cats because people might desire to voice their own opinions, and the consensus is not always easy to come by. Work gets done, but sometimes not as effectively in some situations.

Laissez-Faire Leadership Style

The Laissez-faire leadership style is very different from the previous two styles mentioned. It doesn't ascribe to Theory X or Y. These leaders don't like to control people but also don't guide them. Laissez-faire leaders do the bare minimum. They have a very flippant attitude that what will happen, will happen. Followers can do whatever they want whenever they want without much direction or criticism. This leadership style is most common when an individual is a temporary leader within an organization.

Since laissez-faire leaders are hands-off, this usually results in poor outcomes. Little gets done. Followers tend not to know what to do with little direction and become frustrated. This lack of focus can also cause chaos in the workplace. Productivity, in these cases, takes a nosedive. In some cases, this lack of leadership can spur followers into action to create positive outcomes.

There are specific demographics of followers who can thrive under a laissez-faire leader. Those who need very little in the form of direction and are self-started generally do well when they have individualized tasks that require little supervision and do not need feedback. People who have this type of work ethic tend to be independent contractors.

Visionary Leadership Style

Visionary leaders can see the bigger picture. They are driven innovators who want to impact the world all on their own. They share this vision with others to push their agenda forward to be inspirational rather than be authoritarian. These leaders usually give their employees autonomy to do the job as they wish. This is where the real magic happens because collaboration and innovation can occur in a safe space. Steve Jobs and Elon Musk are a few visionary leaders that have become household names.

A visionary leadership style is most effective when there needs to be an expert of authority in whatever field they're working in and a new vision for the future needs to be created. Additionally, visionary leaders can mobilize people and leverage their expertise to gain the respect and credibility needed for people to follow them. Usually, visionary leadership is successful when you have employees who need more guidance from management.

The great news is that anyone can be a visionary leader. There are a few qualities that all visionary leaders possess regardless of management title:

- persistence
- inspirational
- magnetic
- open-minded
- innovative
- imaginative
- bold and daring
- goal-oriented
- collaborative
- communicative
- organized
- responsible
- enthusiastic
- emotionally intelligent

If you possess these skills, you could implement a visionary leadership style in your organization. These leadership skills could be a game-changer for you. Visionary leaders have all of these skills and more. They can rally others around a vision and lead their company into the future. "A visionary business leader understands that inspiring and motivating employees to embrace the discipline and creativity required to make this vision a reality in turn cultivates greater productivity. And that is excellent for business" (WGU, 2020).

Servant Leadership Style

Robert K. Greenleaf developed servant leadership in 1970. It begins with the innate desire to serve others. This inspires the individual to become a leader. It seems counterproductive but works very well for some people. It's considered to be a non-traditional leadership philosophy. "A servant-leader focuses primarily on the growth and well-being of people and the communities to which they belong" (Robert K. Greenleaf Center for Servant Leadership, 2022).

A servant leader can share the power; they put the needs of employees first and help them succeed. However, this doesn't mean they become a doormat for others. Servant leaders balance the need to help others but not to the detriment of themselves. Instead, servant leaders focus on what they can do to help others become successful and encourage them to have the same servant leadership mindset. Together, everyone achieves more.

This leadership style requires that the leader be altruistic. "Altruism is defined as the belief in or practice of disinterested and selfless concern for the well-being of others" (Wikipedia Contributors, "Servant Leadership"). The leader must possess the desire to want to help other people.

There have been other people who have expanded upon Greenleaf's initial philosophy. James Sipe and Don Frick wrote a book called *The Seven Pillars of Servant Leadership*. This text proposes three key elements that embody servant leadership: motive, mode, and mindset. Their reason for wanting to lead is often radically different from other leadership styles. They truly only want to help other people succeed. They also put others' needs above their own. Finally, they also want others to have the mindset of being servant leaders.

You might be a servant leader if you adhere to the following:

- want to take an other-oriented approach to leadership
- prioritize the needs of others and have meaningful conversations
- care about others, the organization, and the greater community

Choosing Your Leadership Style

Prior to choosing one leadership style that you identify with, take some time to review your workplace. What kind of dynamic currently exists? Is it working? If you believe it could be changed for the better, figure out what can stay the same and what needs improvement. This will help you decide which style fits the followers that currently exist.

You might find that you do not fit into one leadership style. Even the most successful leaders go back and forth between types of followers and situations. You can be flexible and evolve your style as you see fit. There will always be room for improvement. This all goes back to the information from Chapter One. Be self-aware. You'll learn what works for you and what doesn't.

A model will help guide you on your leadership journey if you're not sure what leadership style best fits you. This model is called the Path-Goal Leadership Theory. It requires that an individual chooses a leadership style that best fits the followers and the current work environment. "The goal is to increase your employees' motivation, empowerment, and satisfaction so they become productive members of the organization" (Clark, 2015).

This theory was introduced by Martin Evans in 1970 and further developed by R.J. House in 1971. It's based upon the expectancy theory—the thought that individuals will act in certain ways based on the expectation that their actions are perceived as positive and attractive to others.

The Path-Goal Theory has three basic steps to follow:

1. Figure out what your employee and workplace environment characteristics are.
2. Select a leadership style that fits those characteristics.
3. Shift your focus to motivating others to succeed.

Leadership Training

Leadership training is vital for any organization. It doesn't matter if you have a small or large team; if your team is properly trained, you will see success. Leadership training is a specialized program that helps you and your team learn new techniques and fine-tune any old skills. This training can come in communication, coaching, and other motivational methods you wish to try.

As a leader, you want to have the mindset that you're constantly developing. There are certainly some roadblocks to going back to school to obtain a degree or staffing issues when you must attend class. But, due to being in the golden age of technology, degrees are far more obtainable. There are so many online programs to choose from. However, you can do something to improve company performance if this is not a good fit.

Suppose the company you work for does not already do this. In that case, it's time to design a professional development program that addresses the company's current problems that are a priority. First, work with people internally to encourage learning and team development. These can be simple things like a discussion at a weekly meeting, book clubs, presentations, etc. This can also help pass along skills, frameworks for the business, and company culture. The company could even bring in an external partner for additional training. Short courses could be taken online through companies like Udemy. Another excellent resource for online classes is the Gallup Boss to Coach Course. This can give people administrative and soft skills that bring necessary growth to your organization at an affordable rate.

During your tenure as a leader, you should focus on coaching people to succeed. Pass along the principles, tools, and techniques of your field that will be helpful in the other individual's role. It's important to focus on their natural strengths. Coaching should happen continuously. This also helps to engage those who work with you. It builds the culture, which builds momentum, enthusiasm, and increases productivity.

Leadership for Diverse Groups

Investigate and become familiar with your company's diversity, equity, and inclusion (DEI) policies and commitment.

Working and promoting diverse groups of individuals is vital to the success of any organization. For example: "In 2020, women of color held only 12% of managerial positions, 9% of senior manager/director roles, and 3% of C-suite titles" (Allen & Aweh, 2021). Unfortunately, this has been a challenge within organizations, but it doesn't have to be this way.

Leadership requires you to create a constructive climate and culture; it also requires understanding what diversity and inclusion are. These words take on different meanings, but we'll discuss the textbook definitions in detail. These words tend to bring up many feelings of unfairness, injustice, and exclusion within people. How prepared are you as a leader to address diversity within your organization? How you approach this topic will make or break your success in a leadership role.

Consider the Five Stages of Inclusion when creating a transformative culture (Gundling & Williams, 2021, p.15):

1. Learning About Bias
2. How aware are you of your own biases?
3. How can you learn about others who are different?
4. Building Key Skills
5. What critical skills do you have for being more inclusive?
6. Working Across Boundaries
7. How successful are you in working with diverse groups (gender, generational, functional, cognitive, or cultural diversity)?
8. Becoming a Champion
9. What does it mean to champion inclusion?

10. Do you have what it takes?
11. Getting Results
12. How well do you link inclusion to business results?

Diversity, Equity, and Inclusion (DEI)
Diversity and inclusion have been talked about more in the workplace now than ever before, and for a good reason. These terms are complex. Diversity encompasses a variety of differences that exist amongst groups of people. Diversity in the workplace means creating a space that embraces all walks of life and includes people who may differ from the traditional group within the organization. "Diversity means creating an organizational culture that embraces the values and skills of all of its members" (Northouse, 2021, p. 211). Diversity is more than just a person's race. It also includes social identity. Loden (1996) determined the core dimensions of diversity to include age, race, ethnicity, sexual orientation, gender, and mental and physical abilities (p. 211).

Inclusion goes hand in hand with diversity. "Inclusion is the process of incorporating differing individuals into a group or an organization" (p. 211). This can be done when organizations create a climate and culture accepting of everyone despite differences. "Booysen (2014) suggests that when inclusion exists in a workplace, 'all people from diverse backgrounds will feel valued, respected, and recognized' and 'no one will feel that he or she … does not have a place in the organization; no one will ask: 'What about me?'" (p. 211-212).

Equity is another piece of this puzzle when incorporating diversity and inclusion into your work environment.

It's important to remember that equity is not equality. Equity recognizes that there have historically been inequalities that have kept groups of people from having access to programs, resources, jobs, etc. "Equity aims to provide equal access to resources for historically disadvantaged people" (p. 213). Myers (2012) created a metaphor to help others understand the conversation surrounding DEI: Diversity is about those being invited to the party. Inclusion is being asked to dance. Equity makes sure everyone has the opportunity to dance (p. 213).

Diversity and Inclusion in the Workplace

An organization must address any systemic race and gender issues preventing individuals from being promoted within the organization. Next, an organization can launch a program that specifically focuses on inclusion. This program can combine various leadership training methods previously mentioned, like one-on-one coaching. Career accelerators can be developed for individuals who wish to become a leader within the organization. Do not rule anyone out; remember, anyone can be a leader. You never know what you might be missing out on if you hold limiting beliefs and biases. Many diversity and inclusion courses are available. This type of training is crucial for leading diverse teams and understanding the unique challenges people experience.

As you study your organization's DEI policies and practices, you'll want to find out if they have a model of inclusive practices established. Ferdman (2014) created this model to allow workplaces to have a framework for DEI. There are six components to inclusion: feeling safe, feeling involved and engaged, feeling respected and valued, feeling influential, feeling authentic and whole, and recognizing, attending to, and honoring diversity (p. 223). If all six components are implemented, it gives an organization a great blueprint to work from. Without it, it can create barriers to embracing diversity and inclusion in the workplace.

What does a career accelerator look like? Most have a cohort of participants that learn with each other for at least six months. This program is intended to engage the learners positively to promote growth. Monthly activities of these programs can include:

- one-on-one coaching
- meetings with directors or c-suite members
- workshops
- leadership team meetings

Many successful companies have implemented career accelerators and significantly impacted career progression, hiring, retention, and career navigation.

You might ponder the following advice given by AIChE (2021) when leading diverse teams:

1. Look beyond the exterior. Diversity is so much more than just cultural and racial differences. Teams could be comprised of various ages, genders, religions, socioeconomic backgrounds, and sexual orientations.
2. Go back to your self-awareness. What are your biases? What assumptions do you have about individuals? How can you reduce your biases and create a relationship with people on your team?
3. You must create trust. It all starts with this

component. It's important to establish the ability to have relationships right away and be able to collaborate in the future. This can be done publicly and privately.
4. Keep an open mind. Ask questions. Practice active listening. Others may have different perspectives. Try to integrate these perspectives into the work you do.

Confronting Barriers to DEI

Many things can be potential barriers to the conversation regarding DEI. However, there are five common barriers that you can experience individually and within the workplace: ethnocentrism, prejudice, unconscious bias, stereotypes, and privilege. "Leaders must confront these barriers head-on in order to effectively address diversity and develop inclusion in their organization" (Northouse, 2021, p. 226).

Let us begin by defining some of these terms. They are not ones that easily roll off the tongue and can be challenging to understand. "Ethnocentrism is the tendency for individuals to place their own group (ethnic, racial, or cultural) at the center of their observations of others and the world" (p. 226). This happens when individuals perceive that their culture is better than someone else's culture. It's easy to give our own cultures priority and value them more. It's the failure to recognize other cultures that lead down a destructive path. This can be a large obstacle in the workplace. It's important to remember that:

Leaders need to promote and be confident in their own ways of doing things; on the other hand, they need to be sensitive to the legitimacy of the ways of other cultures.

Skilled leaders are able to negotiate the fine line between trying to overcome ethnocentrism and knowing when to remain grounded in their own cultural values (p. 227).

Prejudice is a barrier as well. "Prejudice is a largely fixed attitude, belief, or emotion held by an individual or group that is based on faulty or unsubstantiated data" (p. 227). These judgments that can be made about people impact the way people treat each other. You can see these prejudices in the systemic discrimination that has happened over time in the policies and practices of organizations across the world.

A less evident barrier is unconscious bias. This is also called implicit bias. This happens when "we have attitudes toward people or associate stereotypes with them without our conscious knowledge that we are doing so" (p. 228). These are the quick judgments we make daily without really knowing it happens. For example, have you ever unconsciously selected interview candidates that matched a particular profile? Have you ever assumed a certain demographic was responsible for the crime? Have you made assumptions about a group of people regarding their mannerisms and behaviors? There is an unconscious bias at play in those moments. One way to avoid these moments is to have ongoing discussions with others from other groups you do not closely identify.

These unconscious biases are often created by stereotypes that have been passed down among generations. "A stereotype is a fixed belief held by an individual that classifies a group of people with a similar characteristic as alike" (p. 229). These labels that are placed on groups are damaging. For instance, have you ever heard someone say that people who work certain shifts are lazy? Or, have you heard someone say a person is good because they are of a certain ethnicity?

The next barrier that's hard to overcome is privilege. It's "an advantage held by a person or group that is based on age, race, ethnicity, gender, class, or some other cultural dimension, which gives those who have it power over those who don't" (p. 230). It's essential to recognize the privilege you possess, especially as a leader. This privilege can skew your perspective. Some people are unaware of their privilege or don't want to admit they have it. They don't understand how that privilege impacts others. Make sure you're not excluding others by using your privilege.

As a leader, you'll have to mitigate these barriers and try to remove as many as possible. The discussion surrounding DEI should include leaders and employees. "Effective leaders recognize the importance of diversity and make it a focal point of their leadership" (p. 231). Take some time to consider the following leadership principles to embrace DEI within your organization.

Top Ten Leadership Principles

There are ten leadership principles that you can focus on to develop for yourself—and they will help others succeed as well. A leadership principle is a belief that every leader should possess. If you don't have these qualities, you may not be able to manage people.

1. Become a role model.
2. Communicate and encourage collaboration.
3. Create a clear and concise vision.

4. Own your mistakes.
5. Be resilient.
6. Limit using power and focus on persuasion.
7. Believe in your mission and vision.
8. Inspire others.
9. Delegate tasks.
10. Embrace innovation to grow.

There are so many leadership styles I have not covered in this chapter, like servant leadership. There are a variety of management styles that can help you become an effective leader. You'll find that most of these styles align closely with the three main leadership styles.

Here is a comprehensive list of management styles you may wish to further research:

- affiliative management
- consensual management
- developmental/coaching management
- directive management
- exemplar/pacesetting management

Reflection Time

1. What leaders have influenced you? What does leadership mean to you?
2. Do you think leaders are born, or is it something everyone can do?
3. How would you rate yourself on the ability to persuade people to follow you?

4. What myths did you believe about management, position, or knowledge?
5. Has your perception of leadership changed?
6. In what ways can you position yourself to learn more about how to influence others? Are there ways to volunteer in your organization or your community?
7. Choose one trait, ability, skill, or behavior that you could improve upon to become a better leader.

3

LEADERSHIP SKILLS FOR THE WORKPLACE

Integrity, insight, and inclusiveness are the three essential qualities of leadership. –Sadhguru

Have you ever stopped to wonder what makes an effective leader? What skills do employers look for in potential leaders? Based on the current research, there are essential leadership skills that one should possess: communication, motivation, positivity, trustworthiness, creativity, feedback, responsibility, commitment, and flexibility. In my honest opinion, communication needs to be your top skill to develop.

"Effective leaders have the ability to communicate well, motivate their team, handle and delegate responsibilities, listen to feedback, and have the flexibility to solve problems in an ever-changing workplace" (Doyle, 2021). You need to be able to communicate clearly and concisely to those you work with. This goes for all communication, whether it be in group settings like meetings, departmental emails, or one-on-one chats no matter the format—phone, email, video, chat, etc. Consistency is key.

Essential Leadership Skills

Leaders should also work to develop their listening skills as a part of their communication development. You need to make yourself readily available to others to discuss issues and concerns that crop up in the workplace. Be sure to study up on the concept of active listening. You will hear this repeatedly in the realm of leadership as it is a valuable skill to master. It involves paying attention to the person speaking by not interrupting and making sure you understand what they're talking about. Don't try to answer their question before you fully understand the entire picture. One way to do this is to not interrupt the person. Wait until they are finished with their thought and then paraphrase what you think they said to show understanding. Look for nonverbal clues and use short affirmations like "I understand" or "I see" as they're speaking to you. You may even want to ask questions that are open-ended or specific to their concern.

Have you ever experienced a workplace where the work becomes boring and employees become complacent? What are the leaders doing wrong around the concept of motivation? Leaders need to inspire people to greatness. There are a variety of ways that leaders can motivate people. It can be intrinsic or extrinsic. You may find that creating a system of recognition and rewards or some other type of recognition is valuable, whereas others will show an increased commitment after giving them new responsibilities. This is the time to really get to know the people you work with. Figure out what makes them tick. What can you do to encourage them to be productive and passionate about what they do?

Here are few ideas to incorporate to increase motivation:

- allowing employees to have more autonomy
- seeking employee input
- surveying employee's personal interests
- mentoring
- setting effective goals
- team-building activities
- recognizing and rewarding employees
- giving a simple thank you
- providing rewarding and challenging tasks

Delegation is another top leadership skill that many leaders fail to take advantage of. Leaders try to do everything and take on too much. This can cause extreme burnout. It also leaves the added risk of tasks not being completed on time or mistakes falling through the cracks. Delegating is not a sign of weakness; it's the opposite. You'll be a stronger leader for allowing others to do tasks for you. It's a sign of trust. Therefore, it's important to know the skills of every person you work with. This allows you, as the leader, to focus on the more important tasks that need your undivided attention.

Some skills that may be helpful while delegating are:

- accepting feedback from others
- giving resources to those who need it to do their job

- focusing on people's strengths and weaknesses (matching them to the right task)
- setting reasonable expectations
- setting SMART goals
- encouraging collaboration and teamwork
- time management
- additional training
- trusting others

Even something as simple as being positive can create a healthy work environment that can help in the long term, even during moments of crisis. People want to work in a positive environment. It's no fun for anyone to be in a negative environment. Positivity will make people want to come to work. This positive mindset can also help during conflict management, developing rapport, being empathetic, and creating respect in the workplace.

None of what we have discussed will come into fruition until you establish trust and respect. This can be done in a variety of ways. Leaders should have the ability to apologize and hold themselves accountable. It also requires a high level of ethics and moral code. Leaders should keep information confidential and be conscientious towards an individual's sensitive information. This will establish trust and credibility when leaders are consistent about doing so. Leaders should also be reliable, respectful, honest, thoughtful, and have integrity.

Innovation in the workplace takes creativity. Leaders need to make sure that their employees have a certain level of autonomy to be able to think outside of the box. For the sake of the organization, the leader must allow for nontraditional ways to solve problems. Some skills that pertain to creative thinking are conceptualization, critical thinking, cognitive flexibility, imagination, innovation, open-mindedness, synthesizing, and collaboration.

Looking back on the importance of communication, feedback is equally important. "Leaders should constantly look for opportunities to deliver useful information to team members about their performance" (Doyle, 2021). This should always be done in a tactful manner. Be clear, but also be empathetic. The feedback will be accepted if it's done in a respectful way. You can give negative feedback, but it's the way you approach it that matters.

Here are some ideas for giving clear feedback:

- be open to receiving feedback yourself
- build confidence in others
- clarity of expectations
- coaching and mentoring
- following up after feedback is given
- listen to the individual's response to your feedback
- positive reinforcement
- give specific advice
- be respectful

Leaders should also hold themselves accountable. Be responsible for both the successes and failures of the team. Don't just blame other people in the process. Accept it, move on and know that there's always room for improvement. Be transparent with those around you. Acknowledging mistakes makes you more human to your team. This also pertains to customer feedback as well. Some things people say will have to be taken with a grain of salt, but it can help you troubleshoot specific areas in the future.

Never overpromise. Follow through with what you say you'll do. This is called commitment. Eventually, those you work with will see your commitment and follow your lead. You cannot expect your team to do their jobs with commitment if you're not also doing the same. This could be something simple like keeping your promises or conveying your passion and determination to accomplish a goal. Embracing professional development also tells your team that you committed to their success in the workplace. Be sure to follow through on what you say. People are always watching and listening. They'll remember when you don't make it a priority.

Leaders need to be open to feedback and suggestions from employees and customers. This requires a certain level of flexibility. Things in the workplace are constantly changing and leaders need to embrace the change. After listening to others' feedback, a leader might be asked or required to learn a new skill or respond to a certain situation. It requires the leader to be adaptable and improvise. It also includes a fair share of negotiation, which we'll spend more time discussing later in our leadership journey.

How to Showcase Your Skills

The easiest way to showcase your skills is by updating your resume. This is the accurate description of your work history. Be sure to incorporate your skills in your cover letter. Many times, people skip over the cover letter. Don't be tempted to do so. This is your opportunity to showcase your skills and have a conversation prior to being selected for an interview. A cover letter allows you to give specific examples where you have demonstrated these skills effectively.

You could hire someone to fine-tune your resume. There are so many recruiters out there that can help you find positions that are a great fit for your skillset. If you haven't made a profile on LinkedIn, hop on over there and do it. Networking is a great way to showcase your skills and show examples of how you're an effective leader.

A great way to showcase your skills on your resume is to provide examples in the job descriptions of your work history. For example, you could mention that you successfully organized meetings, team-building activities, and collaborations with other corporations. It's important to mention these leadership skills throughout the job descriptions. Generic resumes do not convey the level of expertise one may have. A tiny resume gives others the impression that you have poor organizational skills and little experience.

This goes without saying: Prepare for your interviews! Nothing is more embarrassing than stumbling over your words and not remembering key vocabulary that's vital to the job description. Don't wait until the last minute to prepare. You'll want to feel confident and walk through those doors to sell them on your potential.

Here are a few guidelines to follow when choosing leadership examples you wish to showcase during an interview or on your resume:

- Choose a relevant example.

- Choose a recent example.
- Choose an impressive example.

Use the Situation, Task, Action, Result (STAR) method when coming up with potential answers to questions regarding your leadership experiences. What type of situation was it? How did you lead? What was the task? What was the goal? What action did you take? And what was the result?

Now, what if you like your job? What if you want to move up the ranks in your current organization? You'll likely still need to revamp your resume and cover letter, but there are small things you can focus on as well. It's mostly what we have been discussing thus far on this 30-day journey. Practice active listening. Lead by example. Admit that you make mistakes. Be enthusiastic. Be a mentor to those on your team. Be your authentic self. People will notice if you try to become something you're not.

Have you just graduated from college or high school? You might not have a ton of experience. Now is the time to think outside of the box. Here are some examples of leadership experience that may not seem like true leadership:

- leading a project in school
- organizing a group of people (clubs or study groups)
- detecting a problem at work and finding a solution
- working together as a team as an athlete
- volunteer or non-profit work
- training new team members

- leading a meeting or committee
- passion projects (think Eagle Scout projects or Girl Scout Gold Awards)

Improve Your Leadership Skills

There are simple ways to improve your leadership skills. You don't even need to be a leader to develop these skills. The first way to develop your leadership skills is to take initiative. Those who take on more responsibility and tasks at work tend to add more to the work environment. Think about the tasks that would be of most benefit to your department or company. If you do more beyond your daily routine, it could help you out long-term because you're showing initiative.

Requesting more responsibility is another sign that you want to step into a leadership role. Eventually, you'll become the resident expert in your area. How can you help on projects? Lightening the load of your current manager can show that you're interested in expanding your leadership abilities. This also goes together with showing more initiative.

You might want to consider choosing a specific skill to work on. Once you have locked in a skill to improve, you could take a class, read books, set a goal, or find a mentor. The important thing to remember is to create a plan. Create action items to help you improve. Small habits build over time to develop leadership skills.

Critical thinking is one skill that will need to be mastered over time. Effective leaders can see potential issues before they become a larger problem. These leaders have the capacity to prevent them from happening. This is called crisis management. In reverse, these leaders can also detect potential opportunities to leverage them to benefit their organization.

As with most people, active listening skills should be an area to improve upon. Being an effective communicator is crucial to being an effective leader. Without the ability to listen, you will not properly receive feedback from others regarding the project in question. A simple way to work on active listening is to be aware of your actions during a conversation. Are you looking at the speaker? Are you distracted? Be aware of your body language. Do you look interested?

You may also want to learn to be more disciplined within your work. Are you organized? Do you have a vision? Do you have a plan? Be sure to rehearse the presentation when necessary. Communicate effectively and on time. If you are self-disciplined, your followers are more than likely to be disciplined as well. And no, that doesn't mean you need to run a tight ship.

Be willing to be a lifelong learner. The world is an ever changing place and the workplace can change on a dime. Be prepared. Learn a new skill and be willing to be uncomfortable. It might help to study other effective leaders to incorporate some of their qualities or communication styles in your leadership playbook.

Avoid micromanaging your employees. Delegate work to them and give them a level of autonomy to do the work. This will empower them. They will become more involved and develop new skills. This does not mean to brush your hands and walk away from the project if you're the leader or manager. You're still going to be accountable for the product.

Oversee the project in a way that you know tasks are being completed and deadlines are being met. Be sure to communicate what everyone's roles and responsibilities are effectively before the project kicks off.

Know that conflicts will happen. People are people. It's almost inevitable. For the leadership role, you must learn how to handle difficult people and resolve any conflict that comes up. Be sure to talk to people privately and handle issues with integrity. Be honest with them. Don't try to sugarcoat the issue. Some leaders have an issue with being too nice at times. You don't have to be rude, but you do have to be to the point. Being in a managerial role is not always pleasant. There will be times when employees cause a problem that needs to be addressed or the employee should be fired. Gather all the information you can and make an informed decision.

Top Ten Tips for Becoming a Leader

So far, we've discussed transformational leadership, the variety of qualities one must possess to become a leader, and how to develop those skills. Transformational leadership is all about inspiring others to greatness. What can you do to focus on these qualities and become a more effective leader? We discussed this within Chapter Two, but here are some quick strategies to keep at your fingertips.

1. Understand your leadership style. It's crucial that you know what your strengths and weaknesses are. Study up on the major characteristics of your

primary leadership style. Once you figure out what you need to improve upon, devise a plan.
2. Embrace the creative vibes of others. It will help you in the long run to achieve your goals. Encourage others to express their creativity and help with challenges as they arise. Allow people to think outside of the box. You never know what they'll come up with.
3. Be a role model to others. Influence is huge in the realm of leadership. You know the old saying: "Walk the walk and talk the talk." Live it and embrace it. If you want others to do something, then you better be doing it as well. Lead by example.
4. Let your passion and enthusiasm shine! It's not always about getting the job done, it's about having fun and truly believing in the work. Encourage others by giving praise as well as constructive feedback. Let them know how you really appreciate them and the work they do.
5. This next strategy shouldn't surprise you: communicate! Communicate effectively and practice active listening. You'll be more effective when you're able to communicate your overall vision to others and establish trust with them that you're open to communicating. This strategy should be your primary focus to becoming an effective leader.
6. Be optimistic! Positivity can go a long way. It can inspire others to get work done if they're in a positive work environment. Followers will want to

come to work and be excited about the mission. Times of crisis may even feel less daunting due to establishing a positive workplace and culture.

7. Encourage participation from others. Welcome and embrace new ideas. Collaboration is an integral part of effective leadership. It sets the tone for greater commitment, creative problem solving, and increased productivity of those who work within the organization.
8. Motivation is important to inspire others to action. This could very well be the most difficult thing to do as a leader. It doesn't necessarily take a full-blown motivational speech. There are small ways to inspire others. You could be passionate about their ideas or goals. You could help them feel included in the workflow process by giving recognition, praise, or rewards for a job well done.
9. This next strategy builds from the last. Offer rewards or recognition to your staff or followers. People love to be appreciated. Happy people equals better performance.
10. Do not become stagnant. Try new things. People who work for you will have great ideas or feedback on a current project. Listen to them. See what was effective in the past and keep a lookout for new things to try to help inspire others.

Reflection Time

1. What is one area that you can focus on improving in the next 30 days?
2. Have you updated your resume to reflect the new you?
3. What barriers could you face as you try to make these changes to your leadership skills?
4. What will you do to overcome those barriers?
5. What kind of problem solver are you? Are you slow or quick to address issues? What could you do to change this to become an effective problem solver?

4

DEALING WITH THE OUT-GROUP

Not everyone is going to like, approve of, or agree with you or your decisions. And that's okay. –Susan Ritchie

The in-group is the group of individuals that will work with you. They want to embrace your vision and want to help. The out-group may take some convincing and some may never get over that hump. What you do as a leader with the out-group will impact the workplace. Some people view the out-group as being awful, but it doesn't have to be. "Out-groups are common and inevitable, and listening and responding to out-group members is one of the most difficult challenges facing a leader" (Northouse, 2021, p. 252).

It's a delicate balance to appease the out-group. If you fail to meet their needs, out-group members feel like they aren't valued members of the team. As a leader, you need to listen to everybody on the team, not just the ones that suit your needs. It's important to remember that not all out-group members exclude themselves. Think back to the civil rights era or women's suffrage. Some people are excluded intentionally. It will be your job to ensure that never happens in your organization.

You may have been a member of the out-group yourself at one point in time. Have you ever been in a situation where you didn't quite fit in or disagreed with someone else's decision? You were in the out-group if you answered yes. It's a normal part of life and somewhat hard to avoid. So what do you need to do as a leader to help them play ball to get the job done?

Out-group members are those people in an organization that don't conform or identify with the majority group. At times, these individuals can be disconnected and aren't interested in working toward the larger goals of an organization if they have not bought into it. Some people will be more vocal about their opposition, while others may feel like they're alienated, discriminated against, or not accepted by someone or the entire group.

A great leader knows how to leverage the out-group to include them and avoid conflict. Just because they don't agree with your decision or vision doesn't mean they're not able to contribute in a meaningful way. "Out-groups can help prevent groupthink during group decision-making processes by questioning assumptions, resisting pressure to conform to group opinion, and offering alternative perspectives that challenge popular proposals" (p. 253).

Why Do Out-Groups Exist?

There are a variety of reasons why out-groups exist. It could be that people don't agree on a social, political, or ethical stance of the organization's majority group. They can often be seen as the opposition. It could also be explained by social identity theory. "This theory suggests that out-groups come about because some individuals cannot identify with the beliefs, norms, or values of the dominant group members" (p. 254). Out-groups happen when people don't identify with the group and cannot embrace the dominant group's identity for whatever reason.

There is another reason out-groups exist, which is unfortunate and could have been avoided—exclusion. This happens when individuals have a tough time fitting into the group. They may even have poor self-esteem and intentionally exclude themselves. And then, there are situations where people don't fit in and are intentionally excluded by others. This is something, as a leader, you'll want to make sure is avoided in your organization.

Out-groups also exist because of a lack of communication skills or social skills for them to participate in the larger group. The lack of skills alienates these individuals from the majority. Sometimes, these individuals have difficulty filtering what they say or they may act awkwardly. This leaves these people on the outside looking in and some may never be able to adapt to the larger group's norms.

As a leader, you may want to consider coaching these individuals on communication and social skills. It can be an awkward conversation, but if you approach it from a servant leadership perspective, you may be able to gain their trust if you really have their best interest at heart. The out-group requires a certain level of empathy and compassion in leadership.

Showing empathy can be easy to say. But how does one

do it? There are four communication techniques you can implement with the out-group. This is done in conversations that you'll have with people daily. Try restating what they're trying to convey. For example, you might say "I hear you..." or "It sounds like..." The other active listening technique that's useful is paraphrasing. Say in your own words what you think they meant by what they said. Reflection is another technique that helps during conversations. Pay attention to the emotion they convey. You may want to assist them in describing the emotion. In the end, support is what they really need. Let them know that they're not alone.

Out-Groups Do Have Impact

Out-group members can have a positive and negative impact on an organization. Let us get the good, the bad, and the ugly out on the table. It's probably best if we rip the band-aid off and talk about the elephant in the room first.

It's obvious that the out-group can have a negative impact. They can run against what the culture of the company stands for. They can cause conflict by not having the shared vision. They can have a negative impact on the synergy of the group. They can strain relationships. They typically do not garner the respect they deserve from other people.

The good news is the out-group causes leadership to focus on bettering their skills. It causes people to have genuine conversations that can be difficult. Those in the out-group can help improve their communities, especially when dealing with larger societal and ethical issues. It's also an opportunity to embrace a different perspective. As mentioned before, out-group members often exist due to exclusion from the processes that have come before in an organization. Working with the out-group to be 'in' on your leadership and vision can drive true transformation that has buy-in. By appropriately working with and responding to out-group members, they can become some of your strongest in-group members on future initiatives.

Strategies for Responding to the Out-Group

1. Listen to them.
2. Lead with an open mind and tolerance for others.
3. Show empathy to them.
4. Recognize the value they bring to the group.
5. Create a meaningful relationship with them.
6. Give them a voice and empower them.

When the Out-Group Stays Out

Unfortunately, even the best strategies and tactics can only do so much to bring people across the line to support you and your efforts. Sometimes, there will be members of the out-group that will resist and continue to be in opposition to your vision. It's important in these circumstances to continue to follow the strategies above, as no matter what the out-group's position is, they should be treated with respect, given appropriate moments to be heard, and given a voice.

Within the realm of your current initiative, however, you might find that spending a large amount of time on certain individuals in an out-group becomes a poor return on your investment in time and effort. In these circumstances, it's important to reduce risk with this group and find ways to at least isolate their impact on the immediate task at hand. According to the Project Management Body of Knowledge (PMBOK) Guide, there are five major ways that risk can be reduced on a project, and these principles can be applied to working with out-groups that choose to stay out:

1. Escalate: Perhaps you lack the authority to really win over or influence a particular out-group member. In this case, you might choose to escalate that relationship and situation to their manager or other authority.
2. Mitigate: Are there ways to decrease the impact of the person's out-group mentality on the direction of the project?
3. Transfer: This strategy looks and feels a little like escalation in the case of a difficult relationship, but has the nuance of transferring the concern to a third party. Perhaps there's a way to have this out-group member work with a different member of your project team where they feel like their voice can be heard so you can improve buy-in.
4. Avoid: You change your plan to work around the out-group members. Perhaps you have determined the out-group has sufficient influence that your current direction will never get traction with the plan as it is, so you build something new and come at things from a new direction.
5. Accept: You accept that the out-group is what it is,

and that the project plan must continue as is—but you know and are keenly aware that the out-group exists, and you monitor circumstances as they arise.

No matter the direction you choose to go in escalating, mitigating, transferring, avoiding, or accepting risk with your identified out-group, it's again critical to remember that this out-group, no matter how frustrating or challenging they may be—continues to be treated with the utmost respect. Great leaders bring people together and minimize division.

Don't Forget an Out-Group

Maintaining an Enterprise Resource Planning (ERP) platform—systems that help to manage human resources, financials, supply chain, etc.—can be a daunting task. ERP products cover a huge amount of territory. Just by the nature of these products, your stakeholders in implementing and maintaining a platform can be an incredibly exhausting list of effectively every single person in your organization.

In this next story, the project manager had been assigned a new initiative to set up in the existing ERP. There was an opportunity to open up the platform to better serve a key stakeholder group, allowing them to view new information about their clients in a more self-directed manner. However, doing this meant really opening up the platform in some interesting ways that had not been done before—meaning new opportunities for compliance, regulatory, and operational concerns.

Knowing this initiative of providing new data was both critical and setting new precedent, the project manager engaged in a campaign of identifying in-groups and out-groups to see where the situation might go. They worked hard to align the implementation of this new configuration to the best practices of other organizations, worked with strategic leadership across the organization, and developed a seemingly fool-proof plan to provide state of the art information to the stakeholder group.

The new configuration was prepared and launched, with a key announcement sent to the entire organization. That's when the torpedoes started arriving. Seemingly out of nowhere, a new group had identified this solution as being 'unacceptable' and had gone straight to the top of the organization to put a stop to the initiative. The leadership of the organization immediately pulled the plug on the project and it was put aside, with all resources and effort spent on that initiative wasted.

This story does not end there, though, as the project manager knew at some level that the stakeholder group still needed this new configuration and the data it provided. With that in mind, they began a lengthy new approach to work with the out-group members to find common ground and build trust. Ultimately, the out-group that was forgotten in the first attempt of the project found itself requesting that this configuration be put in place and drove the initiative forward to completion.

This story highlights a couple of key major points:

1. Forgetting to really consider all groups, in and

out, up front can be very costly to a leader and the organization they serve.
2. No initiative is truly ever done if you're willing to put in the effort and continue to foster and build relationships. Sometimes it just takes a different approach and a different time to make something happen if you have the vision.

Microaggressions: How to Avoid Them

Microaggressions take place daily whether we are consciously aware of them or not. You might have also heard this term called 'micro-inequities.' No matter what they're called, microaggressions can be verbal, behavioral, or environmental slights. This historically communicates hostile, derogatory, or negative attitudes and beliefs towards groups of people. This concept came to be in 1970 by Chester M. Pierce, who was a psychiatrist working for Harvard University. He developed this term due to what he was witnessing in regard to behavior towards African Americans.

Examples of microaggressions or micro-inequities are:

- gestures
- tone of voice
- word choice
- actions
- unconscious bias

Small behaviors that are usually unconscious lead to bigger issues called macro-inequities. Little things like checking your phone during important conversations or being nicer to one person and not the other are micro-inequities that add up over time; the same goes for work-related behaviors. If you're constantly excluding people from emails, social events, or taking credit for other people's ideas, it can start to take its toll on how people view you. This type of behavior can have a lasting effect on your career.

Here are examples of macro-inequities:

- racism
- sexism
- ageism
- anti-Semitism

This is why inclusive leadership is vital in the workplace. Take the time now to learn about your own biases and work on setting personal boundaries. "Inclusive leadership involves self-awareness, careful listening, outreach to people with different perspectives, and persistent, stubborn efforts to find common ground" (Gundling & Williams, 2021, p. 61-62). Sound familiar?

It's important to create a diverse and inclusive environment for all, not just the elite few. To do this, start with building relationships based upon trust, consistency, and accountability with members of the out-group in a concerted effort to avoid microaggressions. An inclusive environment is relevant for everyone you encounter. Everyone needs to take part in creating that environment, not just leadership. What you do and say matters, and sometimes what you don't say speaks volumes. The following ideas from the University of Washington (2022) are used for micro-support, but it's not exhaustive:

- Give your fullest attention.
- Acknowledge that members of the out-group have strengths and contribute.
- Ask clarifying questions with respect.
- Hold everyone accountable, not just the out-group.
- Break the silence between the in- and the out-groups.
- Do not find a scapegoat to blame.

Common Pitfalls Leaders Make

Too often leaders will rush to someone's rescue, thinking they're being helpful. While you might think your advice is gold, it might not be right for the person's experience or background. This might lead to you solving the problem without really allowing the other person to figure it out for themselves, causing the person to not trust their instincts and creates even more self-doubt. These individuals could stop taking on new roles in the organization due to this type of managerial behavior.

Another common pitfall is letting your own biases or stereotypes get in the way of looking at someone else's skill set. You might assume things that aren't actually true. You might even begin pushing the person to get involved with roles they aren't comfortable with based on an assumption you've made. This could present new challenges for them that they weren't ready for and allow for unfair advantages or disadvantages to take place.

Trends for Inclusion

Gundling and Williams (2021) found six major inclusion trends that are vital when trying to establish an inclusive organizational culture:

1. Awareness to Action: It's one thing to think about inclusion; it's a totally different thing to act upon it.
2. Digitalization and Demographics: In recent years, it has been favored to have bosses who show support for initiatives for inclusion.
3. Global Principles, Local Knowledge: Look at diversity through a local lens. Global concepts are lost on people, whereas if they're familiar with the concept, it will work better.
4. Compliance Challenges: Compliance is important for safety reasons and daily business ethics. It's also important to leverage diversity for product innovation, employee engagement, or new market entry.
5. Competitive Advancement: Research suggests that diversity and inclusion is connected to business benefits.
6. Commitment to Equity: The current conversation is pushing for systemic change. What you do, as an individual and as an organization, can help change the narrative for so many people.

"Inclusion is tied to a 17% increase in team performance, a 20% increase in decision-making quality, and a 29%

increase in team collaboration" (Gundling & Williams, 2021, p. 29). Inclusion is a vital piece of the puzzle for any organization, whether you're dealing with issues of diversity and equity or trying to bring members of the out-group into the fold. Inclusion is a personal responsibility that everyone will need to take. It will help you widen the net and create a climate of 'us' rather than having in- and out-groups. Start by leading with empathy for others and keeping others' perspectives in mind. These leadership lessons are not easy. They will be challenging, but essential. You need to be willing to embrace it. Once you do, you'll be a successful leader.

Reflection Time

1. What strategy will you use to move out-groups in?
2. How can you prevent microaggressions from happening in the workplace?
3. How will you interrupt your own biases?
4. Spend the next five minutes reflecting on your own experiences with micro-aggressions, either as a target or an agent.
5. Who had privilege at that moment?
6. Who were the people marginalized?
7. What type of microaggression happened?
8. Were any shortcuts used?
9. What impact did the event have on those involved?

Now is a great time to start working on your personal action plan as described by Gundling and Williams (2021). Choose at least one of the following areas to study:

- race/ethnicity
- generation
- gender identity
- culture
- job function
- cognitive style
- disability
- sexual orientation
- socioeconomic status
- educational background
- religious belief
- political affiliation
- any other item relevant to your work situation

After you've chosen at least one area to focus on, think about the following questions to create your personal action plan:

1. How can you reach out to meet people from the group(s) you selected?
2. What could you do to learn more about this group?
3. How might you adapt or change your personal style to be more effective when working with this group?

5

NEGOTIATION IN THE WORKPLACE

Let us never negotiate out of fear. But let us never fear to negotiate. –John F. Kennedy

What is Negotiation?

Negotiation is the process people go through to settle differences. It may end in a compromise or some type of agreement to avoid arguments. The goal is to have the result be the best possible outcome for the organization. It's important that, through fairness and maintaining a relationship during these negotiations, some mutual benefit comes out of it. There are three types of negotiators in the world: assertive, accommodator, and analyst. Let's take some time to learn which one you are.

Negotiation is really an art, especially if you're in business. It will be vital to your success. Take some time during this chapter to add some methods to your negotiation game.

Keep your sights on the bigger picture. Sometimes, this means checking your ego at the door. It also means knowing quite a bit about conflict and crisis management. At the end of the day, you will need to seek out a win-win situation and close the deal. A good negotiation can lead to better relationships, long-term quality solutions, and avoid future issues.

Conflict management is a necessary skill for any leader to possess. It's inevitable when dealing with other people. We all have our own opinions and ideas, which can create some challenges. Conflict doesn't always have to mean a full-blown disagreement that causes an internal crisis. Some people believe that conflicts should be avoided at all costs because they're disruptive and cause undue stress. Often, conflict can produce positive changes within an organization. It's okay to be uncomfortable. When effective leaders use their crisis management and negotiation skills, it helps to increase the problem-solving abilities of the staff, strengthen relationships, and decrease stress.

Negotiations should involve a level of compromise between both parties. Those in the negotiation don't necessarily need to meet in the middle to compromise. One side might have more leverage than the other, but it can end amicably and to the betterment of the organization. Negotiations can also be formal and informal. It might be a simple conversation in a meeting, or it could be a written contract.

How you navigate the murky waters of negotiation depends on how you choose to develop your skills over time as well as your interpersonal skills, like how you communicate with others. There are some positions that require negotiation skills: sales, management, marketing, customer service, law, etc. Negotiating a solution should always be the end goal.

As a review, here's a comprehensive list of interpersonal skills that are essential for effective negotiations:

- communication/active listening
- clarification/reducing misunderstandings
- building rapport
- problem solving and decision making
- being assertive
- crisis management
- being able to compromise
- being creative in the ask
- flexibility
- being honest
- presenting it in a tactful way
- showing empathy
- address any misunderstandings
- asking the other party for solutions
- remaining civil

Negotiations can take place when there is not a conflict. Sometimes, you might need to negotiate your next career move with your employer, whether it be a salary increase or title advancement. Most of the time, salary negotiations take place when you're being offered a new job. Some organizations allow for negotiations while others may not. You may also experience the art of negotiation when dealing with union contracts or in freelance and consulting positions.

You may even have to negotiate with your co-workers. If

you work in a team or managerial setting, you must communicate with those you work with. Often, you'll have to negotiate the various roles and workload amongst the team. You may have to ask your employer for a project extension. And, more than likely, you'll have to deal with interpersonal conflicts in the workplace.

Depending on your position, you may have to negotiate with third parties. If you're in sales, it's likely that you will have to negotiate with the client. Even those who work in purchasing need to negotiate contracts to have effective cost savings. Almost every position has some type of negotiating requirement. Some positions like teachers must frequently negotiate with parents, children, and other staff members which can often go unnoticed—whereas everyone knows that a lawyer negotiates daily.

Stages of Negotiation

If negotiation is not your strongest suit, you may want to consider following a structured approach called Best Negotiating Practices (BNPS). This simple structure will lead to building trusting relationships.

The process of BNPS includes the following:

1. Prepare
2. Information exchange and validation
3. Bargain
4. Conclude
5. Execute

You'll want to decide when and where a meeting will

take place to solve the problem in any given negotiation. Who should attend? How long will it take? Have you gathered all the facts? What are the rules of your organization? Will they impact the outcome? Some organizations have policies in place that impact how you prepare. This might seem like a waste of time to some, but it allows you to avoid any further conflict.

At the beginning of the discussion, each person involved should be able to present their case and how they understand the situation. Here is where, as a leader, you'll need to hone in on your questioning, listening, and clarifying skills. You may want to consider taking notes that you can refer to. Once a civil conversation has taken place, each person's goal or viewpoint must be clarified to move forward. Without clarification, misunderstandings can cause even further issues to reach an outcome.

During the exchange stage, you'll want to look at the four critical assessments: trustworthiness, competency, likability, and alignment of interests. If the person is honest and dependable, there's the potential for you both to work together for a suitable outcome, especially if your interests align with theirs. Sometimes, the negotiation process can be negative, so you'll need to make adjustments to your Best Alternative to a Negotiated Agreement (BANTA).

Hopefully, through this process, both parties can move towards a win-win outcome. This is when both parties feel like they have gained something positive during the negotiation and feel like they have been heard. This is the best-case scenario. It may not always be possible, but this is the true purpose of negotiation. If an acceptable solution has been agreed upon, the agreement should be clear so those involved understand the final decision.

You wouldn't want to end up like Henry Clay, "The Great Compromiser." Clay was a politician in the 1770s that had an incredible career as the Speaker of the House and had a knack for negotiation. He was very influential in passing the Missouri Compromise of 1820. This balance of power between free and slave states won Clay the title of being "The Great Compromiser." Even though he always wanted to bring people together through compromise, he wasn't one to shy away from airing his grievances, and he always wanted what was the best outcome for all. There were some who opposed him because they wanted to win whatever negotiation was being sought after. This caused Clay to lose many presidential elections because those who opposed him were concerned that he would pose a problem to their end game.

Now, if you are one of those people that like to drive a hard bargain and want to always achieve that 'yes' you're seeking in a negotiation, you might want to follow Roger Fisher and William Ury's method called principled negotiation (1991). Within this method, there are four principles: people, interests, options, and criteria. This model suggests that you need to separate people from the problem. They suggest that you put yourself in their shoes to gain perspective of the situation. This allows you to focus on interests and not positions. They believe that focusing on positions gets you nowhere. Once you focus on interests, it allows for the opportunity to invent options that are for mutual gain. Communication is key in these situations. You'll need to be an active listener to get what you want out of the negotiation.

If you insist on using objective criteria, it will result in a yes. There's usually more than one criterion as a basis for an agreement to take place. Be fair in your standards. Be sure that the negotiation process is also fair. This means taking turns when speaking, flipping a coin, and so on. Mediation also is a way to establish fairness in negotiation. Sometimes, fairness is also taking company policy into consideration.

Ways to Approach Conflict

Unfortunately, there are some cases where an agreement cannot be reached. This usually takes place if the process of the negotiation goes south. If you notice that parties in the negotiation are starting to break down and become frustrated, reschedule the meeting for a different time to have further discussions. This can prevent a heated discussion or argument taking place unnecessarily. It's best to try to salvage a relationship before things get too heated. Rescheduling the meeting can also allow for both parties to find alternative solutions or seek mediation for the next meeting.

Schmidt and Tannenbaum (1960) claimed there is no right or wrong way to deal with issues pertaining to differences. The most commonly used communication strategies are differentiation, fractionation, and face-saving. Differentiation usually happens early on in a disagreement. It helps you establish your position or stance on a given issue and it helps both parties see each other's point of view. Fractionation helps to break down large conflicts into sizable chunks. It makes the issue more manageable. Face-saving is a valuable skill in negotiations because it helps people maintain their image. It's important to protect your image in moments of conflict.

There are different ways to handle conflict and those styles will impact the outcome. "A conflict style is defined as a patterned response or behavior that people use when approaching conflict" (Northouse, 2021, p. 293). Kilmann and Thomas (1975, 1977) developed a model that identifies five conflict styles based upon the work of Blake and Mouton (1964). The Kilmann-Thomas model conflict styles are avoidance, competition, accommodation, compromise, and collaboration. This model splits the styles into two dimensions: assertiveness and cooperativeness. Assertiveness takes place when individuals want to satisfy their own concerns, whereas cooperativeness is when the negotiation satisfies both parties.

Avoidance

The avoidance style fits into both the unassertive and uncooperative style. People who like this style tend to be passive and ignore conflict solutions instead of dealing with them head-on. You might consider these individuals to be in a state of denial. These individuals are not interested in pushing their own agenda or helping others push theirs. This style is counterproductive in the workplace because it can lead to even more stress and conflict. It can also cause the person avoiding the conflict to bottle it up, which can quickly escalate in the future if unleashed. There are a few times where avoidance may be beneficial. If there is a situation that's trivial or if the damage of a conflict could be too great, avoidance may provide the space for both parties to cool off and deal with a solution later.

Competition

Competition is used when individuals are highly assertive about their own goals and interests. They're often uncooperative in helping others achieve theirs. Typically, you see this in the workplace when people are trying to control or persuade others to do their bidding. This style is a win-lose strategy. The only time competition can be beneficial is when a quick decision needs to be made. For some, competition can generate more creativity and enhance performance for those who need a challenge. Most of the time, however, it can be counterproductive and cause additional conflict in the workplace in the form of winners and losers.

Accommodation

The conflict style of accommodation is an unassertive but cooperative type. In this process, the individual communicates with the other person and effectively says that they agree with them; it's others oriented. By using this style, problems are confronted rather than deflected. This style helps people move from being uncomfortable in moments of conflict. The goal for this style is to be productive and create harmony in the workplace. Some people can view this style as being a lose-win strategy because it can come at the sacrifice of the individuals' goals or ideas. It's a submissive way to deal with conflict. This can become a problem if an individual always sacrifices themselves constantly to avoid conflict.

Compromise

A compromise takes place somewhere between competition and accommodation. It has equal levels of assertiveness and cooperativeness. This is often known as "give and take" in the workplace. It's a mix of accommodating your own needs and others. The conflict is not necessarily avoided, but it doesn't result in a massive argument, either. Ultimately, compromise can produce positive results. People must work together to come to a consensus. It gives equal power to both parties to come to a solution. Unfortunately, some people can view this as taking the easy way out. This is because each party does not really get to air all their grievances to work together.

Collaboration

The last style is collaboration. This is the best style of conflict. It's both assertive and cooperative. In this situation, both parties come to an agreement that's best for both. It also doesn't sacrifice anything amongst the parties. "Collaboration is the ideal conflict style because it recognizes the inevitability of human conflict. It confronts conflict, and then uses conflict to produce constructive outcomes" (p. 296). Therefore, most workplaces prefer the use of collaboration. It's a win-win. Communication is amplified, relationships are strengthened, and it can be more cost-effective when a solution is determined. It does take some effort to sustain, but it produces the most desirable results if all parties are willing to work together.

Top Ten Negotiation Skills

Now that you know what negotiation is and what it looks like, the Harvard Law School (2021) has devised a list of the top ten negotiation skills you need to learn to succeed at integrative negotiation.

1. Analyze and cultivate your BATNA (Best Alternative To a Negotiated Agreement).
2. Negotiate the process.
3. Build rapport.
4. Listen actively.
5. Ask good questions.
6. Search for smart trade-offs.
7. Be aware of the anchoring bias.
8. Present multiple equivalent offers simultaneously (MESOs).
9. Try a contingent contact.
10. Plan for the implementation stage.

How to Protect Yourself During a Negotiation

Remember Harvard's number one negotiation skill? Know your BATNA well. What results are you looking for during a negotiation? What are the other alternatives? A BATNA is your only defense that "can protect you both from accepting terms that are too unfavorable and from rejecting terms it would be in your best interest to accept" (Fisher & Ury, 1991, p. 100). Having an alternative plan can reduce your own pressures, minimize your chances of accepting a not-so-great offer, and help you set realistic goals and expectations for what you want to achieve. Another way to protect yourself from accepting terms that aren't acceptable to you would be to ask for some time to consider it or ask for a mediator at the next meeting. This will give you some wiggle room.

Make sure that you never enter a negotiation on the defensive. It could come back to haunt you. By defending your ideas, you'll invite criticism or advice depending on the person you're negotiating with. If the individual does attack you, resist the urge to fight back. Let them air their grievances and then redirect their attack towards the problem. It will also benefit you to be an active listener in this process. Wait until the other person is done speaking so as to not cut them off. This will also help avoid further conflict.

In some cases, the person you are negotiating with can drive a hard bargain and not play fair. "Tricky bargaining tactics are in effect one-sided proposals about negotiating procedure, about the negotiating game that the parties are going to play" (p. 130). What do you do? The simple answer is to counter them. You'll have to redefine the rules of the game. You may need to come at the negotiation from a different angle. You may even have to call to question the tactic's legitimacy. Fisher and Fry's main method of negotiation still applies after you have redirected the situation.

Here is a quick list of common tricky tactics from Fisher and Fry (1991):

- Deliberate deception
- phony facts
- ambiguous authority
- dubious intentions
- Psychological warfare
- stressful situations
- personal attacks
- good guy versus bad guy routine
- threats
- Personal pressure tactics
- refusal to negotiate
- extreme demands

- escalating demands
- lock-in tactics
- hardhearted partner
- calculated delay
- "take it or leave it" stance

If the negotiation goes south and a mediator is needed, make sure that the third-party mediator can create and establish a constructive environment where you both can discuss, propose, and resolve issues fairly and objectively. Without this equal footing, the negotiation is bound to be headed for disaster again.

Be sure to brush up on your company's policy regarding dispute resolutions. Many companies have a guide that defines the best practice for dispute resolution processes. A guide should recommend that issues be solved quickly rather than letting issues escalate. It should recommend that all parties include all sides to the story to create fairness. These disputes should be handled with sensitivity, keep things confidential to protect all parties, and the process should be transparent. The policies and procedures to dispute resolutions should be clear to every employee, regardless of level.

Reflection Time

As part of your reflection time, take a paraphrased look at Fisher and Fry (1991)'s ten questions people ask about getting to 'yes':

1. Does positional bargaining make sense?

2. What if we can't agree on what's fair?
3. Should I be fair?
4. What if the person is the problem?
5. Should I negotiate with a terrorist?
6. Should I adjust my approach to accommodate for differences of personality, gender, or culture?
7. How do I decide what tactics to use? Like, where should we meet?
8. How do I go from inventing options to making commitments?
9. How much risk should I take?
10. How can I improve my negotiating power?

So, now that you've had time to digest all of that, let's contemplate the following question...

Think back to a situation where negotiation was needed. How did you separate the person from the problem? Were you able to work together? Were you able to take their perspective into account? What was the result?

6

TEAM MANAGEMENT

Leaders are people who do the right things; managers are people who do things right. –Warren G. Bennis

Congratulations! You've just landed your first managerial role with the company. What do you do now?

As discussed in previous chapters, a leader must create a vision and manage tasks and people to accomplish their goals. This cannot be done without establishing a constructive climate for your organization or team. The climate is the atmosphere of a team or organization. It's defined by the perception of the way things are going or how people feel about the activity, procedures, or assumptions (Northouse, 2021, p. 182).

It will be important for you to study your organization's current climate to assess whether change needs to take place and find your place in the current climate. "In order to create a constructive climate, a leader needs to consider four factors: providing structure, clarifying norms, building cohesiveness, and promoting standards of excellence" (p. 183).

No one likes working in utter chaos. Therefore, structure is needed for your team. This gives people meaning and purpose to the activities they'll be doing. It also provides stability, security, and direction for those who are unsure of how to perform. You'll need to constantly communicate with your team and give them specific tasks. Be sure to get to know everyone on your team and what they bring to the table. This can help create synergy when everyone knows their role and how they can contribute to the group.

Clarification of norms will be something you'll want to do to create a positive climate. "Norms are the rules of behavior that are established and shared by group members" (p. 184). This provides a guide to those you work with on how to behave in a group. It's important to know that norms don't just emerge on their own. They need to be established at the beginning through interactions with the leader and the team. These norms are important because they'll dictate how things operate in the future.

Another way to establish a successful climate is to focus on the team's cohesiveness. This is the glue that holds everyone together. It creates a safe space for people on the team to express themselves and gives people the ability to give and receive feedback. It's important to have an environment where people can share their ideas and opinions even if they're different from others on the team, thus creating a climate where people feel accepted.

There are several things you can do to build a cohesive team. Build your leadership skills by doing the following:

- Create a climate of trust.
- Provide a vision and purpose.
- Set clear goals and expectations.
- Lead by example.
- Be optimistic and positive.
- Encourage people to be active participants.
- Encourage teamwork.
- Help others achieve their goals.
- Create a safe space where people can share their thoughts.
- Delegate leadership responsibilities to others.
- Give praise often.
- Communicate, communicate, communicate.

Motivation is Key

Looking back at Theory X and Theory Y that was previously discussed, those theories provide two very different ways to motivate your team. How do you view the people on your team? Do you think they're lazy? You might lean towards Theory X. Do you think they're happy to work? If so, you likely align with Theory Y.

Not sure how to motivate people? You might need motivation yourself. There are several approaches to motivating others. The approaches are simple and incredibly effective. Let's look at the three most common approaches to motivating others in the workplace.

Herzberg's Motivation-Hygiene Theory

Frederick Irving Herzberg was an American psychologist who developed the Motivator-Hygiene Theory. This theory divides motivation into two categories: motivators and hygiene factors. These categories are crucial to motivation in the workplace; motivators are associated with job satisfaction and hygiene prevents job dissatisfaction.

There are six motivator or intrinsic factors in Herzberg's Motivation-Hygiene Theory:

- achievement
- recognition
- growth
- advancement
- responsibility
- the work itself

There are ten hygiene or extrinsic factors in Herzberg's Motivation-Hygiene Theory:

- company policies and administration
- quality of technical supervision
- quality of interpersonal relations with co-workers, subordinates, and superiors
- job security
- working condition
- status or position at work
- personal life

This theory is like Maslow's Hierarchy of Needs. The two men conducted their research around the same time. Herzberg built upon Maslow's theory to address motivation in the workplace. What he found was that there was a lack of linear relationship between the two needs, intrinsic and extrinsic. This caused Herzberg to change his factors to discover both the satisfiers and dissatisfiers in the workplace. If the basic needs are met in the workplace, then it's more likely to increase the attitudes and motivation of an individual.

McClelland's Human Motivation Theory

In 1961, David McClelland, another American psychologist, developed the Human Motivation Theory. This theory continues to be a great resource for leaders and managers in the business field today. This theory is also known as the Three Needs Theory or Acquired Needs Theory, depending on where you look.

This theory has three main motivational drivers or needs that everyone has. One of those drivers is the dominant motivator. It's important to note that these drivers or needs are acquired over time. They aren't something you're born with; they are results of our experiences in the world.

The three drivers are a need for achievement, affiliation, and power. Of course, these will vary for everyone depending on your dominant driver, but everyone should find a place within the three. As you study this theory, try to figure out which is your dominant driver and where your team would fall to understand them better. If you can figure out someone's dominant factor, it will help you to set goals, provide meaningful feedback, and reward and motivate them.

Factor #1—Achievement:

- strong desire to set and achieve goals
- take risks to accomplish goals

- works well with others
- high achievers
- can give and receive feedback well
- motivated by accomplishments
- completes projects
- good leaders
- have high expectations
- can be demanding

Factor #2—Affiliation:

- Loves being a part of a group
- Loves to be liked
- agreeable
- cooperative
- does not like taking risks
- does not seek praise
- loves interacting with people
- happier in non-leadership roles
- optimal performers
- loves harmony in the workplace

Factor #3—Power:

- desires power
- wants to have control over others
- wants to be influential
- loves competition
- enjoys status and recognition
- can be argumentative
- will do anything to win

- great for achieving company objectives

Sirota's Three Factor Theory

As the name suggests, there are three factors in the Three Factor Theory: equity and fairness, achievement, and camaraderie. These three factors can be vital to your team's ability to build enthusiasm. Sirota developed this theory to change the conversation from how to motivate employees to how to keep management from destroying employee's motivation. The survey Dr. Sirota administered had four modes of relationships with employees. In culture, it included partnership, paternalistic, adversarial, and transactional. In relationships, it included allies, children, enemies, and ciphers.

This theory is simplistic because everyone desires a workplace that promotes fairness. People enjoy accomplishing things and having positive relationships with others—it's a no-brainer. These factors are all universally positive attributes to focus on. When you can have these three factors work together in business, it can be beneficial to your organization.

Sirota's Three Factor Theory goes back to everything we've discussed thus far. Create fairness in the workplace by creating a fair work volume and employee compensation package. People thrive in environments where they have job security and consistency. You'll also want to make sure the work is challenging enough for them to stay motivated. The work needs to involve tasks or projects that are achievable, however. Be sure to allow your employees to have the necessary resources to get the job done. And, in the end, if you create a climate that encourages cooperation and teamwork, those who work for you will want to stay.

This theory is best represented as a funnel. All three factors flow down the funnel to create a successful work environment. This is accomplished when everyone has a need to feel a sense of achievement when a challenge is presented and the efforts are recognized. Everyone must have the same goals. The organization needs to fulfill the primary needs of the employee. Ultimately, the employee needs to be motivated to complete the work.

Management Styles: Pros and Cons

In this section, we'll revisit some of the types of leadership styles. The terms "leadership styles" and "management styles" are sometimes used interchangeably. Although, some would argue that they're entirely two different things. It depends on who you talk to. All joking aside, you really need to pay attention to what style you ascribe to. "Over 50 percent of Americans have left a job to get away from a manager" (Brown, 2021). For the sake of time, we will look at the pros and cons of the styles we have already discussed: autocratic, democratic, laissez-faire, visionary, and servant leadership.

Autocratic Management Style

Managers who ascribe to this management style seek to control all decisions. These individuals barely take any input from others or the group. Employees rarely like a manager who fits into this management style.

Pros:

- great for quick decision making

- streamlined processes because one person does it all
- under-performance is not tolerated

Cons:

- does not encourage cooperation or delegation
- decision making is difficult when the manager is not available
- turnover rates increase

Democratic Management Style

The democratic management style requires collaboration from both the manager and the team. This allows power to be distributed amongst the team and encourages every member to be a part of the decision-making process. These leaders tend to be inclusive and create a safe space for dialogue to occur. In the end, this produces a team that has better performance.

Pros:

- strong working relationships
- allows for complex issues to be solved
- team knowledge increases
- encourages innovations
- everyone benefits

Cons:

- decision-making process can be drawn out

- can cause tension when not implemented correctly
- leader can lose control quickly due to lack of structure

Laissez-Faire Management Style

This style is known for the delegation that takes place between management and their team. All decision making is passed off to the team and the manager takes a hands-off approach. The team is left to their own devices and receives very little guidance from management.

Pros:

- team become the resident experts
- fosters a creative workplace
- employees feel trusted
- boosts staff morale
- employees take ownership of the work

Cons:

- leaders appear to be lazy
- employees can become confused with lack of structure
- can result in poor performance
- management can have a hard time implementing changes due to autonomy that's been previously given

Servant Leadership Management Style

A person who's ascribed to the servant leadership management style looks for ways to serve those who are on their team. This doesn't mean you cater to their every whim. It allows you to find ways to motivate others to achieve their goals, which will ultimately lead to the organization's success.

Pros:

- grows people
- allows for open communication
- everyone achieves
- relationships become stronger
- employees felt heard

Cons:

- some people may not be as self-directed
- takes time to implement
- not tailored towards a quota-driven environment

Visionary Management Style

By using the visionary management style, the manager can focus on the bigger picture. This bigger picture helps to guide problem solving processes and initiatives that are selected. It can be more hands-off because the employees are trusted to do the work that leads the organization to its vision.

Pros:

- team believes in the work
- more team engagement
- ideas easily shared

- employees become invested
- lowers employee turnover

Cons:

- lack of vision can halt progress
- leader or manager isn't inspiring

Now that we've covered the pros and cons of each management style, you'll want to consider the following questions when figuring out which style is right for you and your team.

1. How much time is needed for the project?
2. What skills or qualities will need to exist on the team?
3. Who will need feedback?
4. How much time has a person been on the job?
5. How much work can you delegate?
6. What is your overall vision? What is the result you want?
7. Who is your target audience? How will they receive the results?

As you reflect on the different management styles and questions, you may want to consider looking for some aptitude tests online to get an idea of which style would suit your personality. The Myers-Briggs Type Indicator is a great place to start. This can help you figure out your own personality as well as your team's and how that personality is perceived by others.

The 360 Leadership Assessment is another tool to help you. Leadership Circle has a variety of instruments that can help you gain insight into those around you and develop a plan for your leadership development. Don't confuse these leadership assessments with an employee assessment. These tools are meant for employees to receive feedback from all stakeholders who work with them. They help individuals become more self-aware.

While there is no right leadership style, there are ones that better suit certain situations and personalities. Different people will respond to the various styles in different ways. This is normal. Different tasks will also require certain styles. The important thing to remember is that knowing your team and communicating with them are essential to your success as a leader and manager.

Micromanagement versus Macromanagement

"A micromanager is a boss or manager who gives excessive supervision to employees" (Kagan, 2021). These types of managers have a tendency to tell employees how to do their jobs. They watch employees very closely and critique everything. This style works in the short-term to get things done. Unfortunately, over time, these types of managers end up causing a hostile environment and the climate starts to decline. People begin to resent the manager and feel like they don't trust them to get the job done.

Micromanagers waste a long time worrying about what others are doing instead of doing more important things. They also don't see themselves as micromanaging others.

Are you showing signs of micromanagement in your management style?

Here are signs of micromanagement:

- requesting to be CC'd on every email
- asking for constant updates
- worrying about other people and how they are working
- looking over people's shoulders to monitor them
- wanting to know what people are always doing
- never being satisfied with what people produce
- focusing on the wrong details

Are you a micromanager? Do you know a micromanager? Can they be reformed? There are a few things you can do to help yourself or others break the cycle. When dealing with a project, set a couple of objectives or SMART goals that can define successful completion. It's important to delegate what needs to be done, but don't tell others how to do it. Communication is also essential. Keep an open door policy if the team needs help. And, of course, be sure to set a deadline for the project. This should be a reasonable timeline that everyone can be successful with. You can even request updates as people work to stay in the loop, but it's not something you harp on someone to receive.

On the flip side, "a macromanager is a type of boss or supervisor who takes a more hands-off approach and lets employees do their jobs with minimal direct supervision" (Hayes, 2021). This can be a mixed bag for some. Macromanagers sometimes get a bad rap for not giving their employees enough support or feedback to do their jobs. And, for others, this freedom is welcomed. These types of managers care more about the overall picture rather than the nuts and bolts that get them there.

Macromanagement is a top-down approach. The person at the top watches carefully as tasks and decisions are delegated downstream. This style allows employees to have more autonomy, but it can also have its downfalls as well. These types of managers can appear to be cold and distant to employees, even if that's not the image they want to portray. If a manager is not aware of the day-to-day operations, they may not understand how a task should be performed. This can get annoying to the person doing the task, especially if the manager is giving them feedback.

In the end, you'll need to keep your eyes on the prize. What are you trying to accomplish? How will you get there? Frame your ideas in such a way that others can envision them. Language is important when framing things. Some people might interpret the connotations incorrectly, which can take you down the wrong path. Communicate often and early and give constructive feedback while also being affirming. This can be a daunting task for some. It's a tap dance that needs to be rehearsed before performing.

Reflection Time

Let's take some time to ponder some potential questions you might be asked to answer during an interview for a leadership or management position.

1. Can you describe your biggest accomplishment and failure in your current or previous role?

2. What is your management style? How do you think this will fit in our organization?
3. Explain a time when you had to make a difficult decision in a previous role.
4. How do you deal under pressure or in stressful situations?
5. How do you delegate work to others?
6. How do you motivate others?
7. Where do you see yourself in the next ten years?

7

EMOTIONAL INTELLIGENCE

When dealing with people, remember you are not dealing with creatures of logic, but with creatures of emotion. –Dale Carnegie

Emotional intelligence is a topic within the realm of leadership that you don't want to overlook. Margaret Andrews, an instructor of emotional intelligence in leadership, says, "Emotional intelligence is critical in building and maintaining relationships and influencing others—key skills that help people throughout their career and wherever they sit in an organizational structure" (Harvard Professional Development, 2019). Emotional intelligence has been linked to people being more innovative and having higher job satisfaction. It will be important for you to learn what emotional intelligence is all about and how you can improve your skills to set yourself up for success.

Before we dive in, here's a quick history lesson about how emotional intelligence came to be.

The term emotional intelligence was not coined until the 1990s. The concept, however, has been around much longer than that. In the 1930s, psychologist Edward Thorndike, developed the concept of social intelligence. This occurs when people have the ability to get along with one another. David Wechsler took this a step further in the 1940s and claimed that there were different components of intelligence that factored into one's success in life.

Fast forward to the 1950s: Maslow developed his hierarchy of basic needs. From this came several other theories, including Gardner's multiple intelligences. This concept confirmed that there was more than just one ability in intelligence. The term emotional intelligence started cropping up in the mid 80s; first in a dissertation by Wayne Payne.

Now that you know the humble beginnings of emotional intelligence theory, what is it exactly?

What is Emotional Intelligence?

The term emotional intelligence (EQ), also known as emotional quotient, originated in the 1990s by two researchers named John Mayer and Peter Salovey. "Emotional Intelligence (EQ) is defined as the ability to identify, assess, and control one's own emotions, the emotions of others, and that of groups" (Coaching Direct). In 1996, Daniel Goleman, a psychologist, took the idea of emotional intelligence and discussed why emotional intelligence means more than your IQ does. There are four attributes commonly associated with emotional intelligence: self-management, self-awareness, social awareness, and relationship management.

Those who have low EQ often feel misunderstood and get upset very easily. They become overwhelmed by their emotions. They also have difficulty with being assertive. On the flip side, those who have a high EQ understand that there's a connection between their emotions and how they behave. These individuals can remain calm and collected in stressful environments and situations. They can influence and motivate people towards a shared goal. They don't have any issues with being assertive and they can handle difficult people professionally.

There are two types of tests that can assess the levels of emotional intelligence one possesses: self-report tests and ability tests. The most common type of tests are self-report tests. They are easy to administer and score. People like simple things; it allows the individual to rate their own behaviors. Have you ever taken a test that asks if you disagree, somewhat disagree, agree, or strongly agree? If you said yes, then you've taken a self-report test. Ability tests involve having people respond to certain situations and then assessing their skills. This usually is rated by a third party.

You can even have your emotional intelligence measured by a mental health professional, and this will be more accurate than something you find online. The two measures are called the Mayer-Salovey-Caruso Emotional Intelligence Test (MSCEIT) and the Emotional and Social Competence Inventory (ESCI). The MSCEIT is an ability test that measures the four branches of Mayer and Salovey's EI model: perception of emotion, the ability to reason using emotions, the ability to understand emotion, and the ability to manage emotions. The ESCI is an older tool that's also called the Self-Assessment Questionnaire. This tool allows individuals to rate themselves on different emotional competencies.

Let's take a closer look at Mayer and Salovey's Emotional Intelligence Model...

First, you need to be able to perceive emotions accurately. This includes watching for nonverbal signals like body language and expressions. If you can do this with ease, you can move on to the second step, which is reasoning with emotions. You need to recognize the role emotions play when promoting thinking and cognitive activity. Pay close attention to others' emotions and how you react to them.

The third step is understanding emotions. As we all know, emotions have a wide range of meaning and can be interpreted in various ways by different people. There are some universal meanings to emotions. For instance, if your co-worker is angry at work, it could be because he's upset with the workload or he got into a fight with someone at home. The last step is managing emotions. This part is integral and involves a higher level of emotional intelligence. You must have the ability to regulate your own emotions and respond to others' emotions appropriately.

Another emotional intelligence theory is the Bar-On Model of Emotional-Social Intelligence. Reuven Bar-On, an Israeli psychologist, developed the model in 2006. "The Model consists of five interrelated competencies, skills, and behavior clusters that were identified from academic literature" (Moore, 2022). The clusters are self-awareness and self-expression; social awareness and interpersonal relationships; emotional management and regulation; change management; and self-motivation (Moore, 2022). This model suggests that our EQ competencies and skills influence how other people see and understand us.

If you're familiar with emotional intelligence theories, you've probably heard the name Daniel Goleman. His work is synonymous with emotional intelligence skills. This theorist is widely used in the world of leadership and business. Goleman's model is an extension of Mayer and Salovey's work. Goleman's model has five factors that determine a person's emotional intelligence: emotional self-awareness, self-regulation, motivation, empathy, and social skills.

The work of Goleman on emotional intelligence and communication skills highlights the importance of EQ in the workplace, especially in the realm of leadership. Goleman pointed out that when you work in high IQ labor markets, people who have soft skills stand out (Moore, 2022). This is a good thing!

"The Center for Creative Leadership even draws on research to suggest that 75% of careers are negatively impacted by emotional competency-related themes. These include the inability to respond adaptively to change, nurture trust, lead teams during tough times, and deal effectively with interpersonal problems" (Moore, 2022).

Now that we know the theory behind it, what do emotional intelligence skills look like? We know they take place every day in our lives. But have you really stopped to pay attention to them?

1. Listen to others.
2. Drive communication at a higher-level.
3. Understand others' perspectives.

Why is Emotional Intelligence Important?

Over the years, many researchers have suggested that emotional intelligence can be learned and built upon, while some claim that you're born with it. We all know that being able to express and control our emotions is vital, especially when working with other people. It's equally important that we know how to read other people's emotions and respond to them appropriately.

In recent years, there's been a push to teach social and emotional intelligence, especially in the school setting. This helps children improve their health, well-being, and academics, and it prevents bullying as well. These skills are essential to learn at a young age because they can play a role in your daily life, especially in the workplace.

Have you ever worked with someone who was brilliant yet lacked social skills? Did this impact their ability to work with others or lead? Probably so. These individuals can be frustrating to communicate with. It just goes to show that your IQ (intelligence quotient) is not enough to be successful in life. Without emotional intelligence, you are unlikely to manage your emotions or stressors in your life or communicate effectively with others.

Emotionally intelligent people are:

- Able to think before reacting.
- Able to know that emotions are powerful and temporary.
- Good at thinking about how others must feel.
- Aware of their own feelings.
- Empathetic towards others.

- Able to resolve conflicts.
- Able to coach and motivate others.
- Able to create a culture of collaboration.
- Able to build a safe work environment.

You may be wondering if you know where you land in the scheme of emotional intelligence. Luckily for you, there are emotional intelligence skills assessments that are readily available. These will help you measure your emotional intelligence. Be leery of any assessment you find on the internet. Not all are valid. The two official emotional intelligence skills assessments are the Mayer-Salovey-Caruso Emotional Intelligence Test and the Harvard Business Review EQ Assessment.

EQ Matters More Than IQ

There are many reasons why EQ is more important than IQ. One of the biggest reasons is that emotional intelligence is essential for communication. If you can understand emotions, it will help you build better relationships and create stronger communication skills. "There is no known connection between IQ and EQ; you simply can't predict EQ based on how smart someone is. Cognitive intelligence, or IQ, is not flexible" (Bradberry & Greaves, 2012, p. 131).

Your emotional intelligence affects many aspects of your life. Take, for instance, work or school. Having a high emotional intelligence can help you figure out the complexities of your social network. It also helps you have the ability to lead or motivate other people. It's common now for employers to ask you to take a test measuring your emotional intelligence as part of the interview process.

"The daily challenge of dealing effectively with emotions is critical to leadership because our brains are hardwired to give emotions the upper hand" (Bradberry & Greaves, 2012, p. 129). Due to this, you have no control over the process. When something happens, you'll have an emotional reaction. As you develop your EQ skills, you'll figure out what triggers you and what doesn't. You'll need to learn different strategies to have productive responses to those triggers.

Your emotional intelligence also affects your physical and mental health. If you have a lower EQ, it's likely that you cannot regulate your emotions or your stress. This could lead to health issues like a compromised immune system or high blood pressure. It could also lead to anxiety or depression. All of this will have an impact on your personal and work-related relationships. Working on your emotional intelligence will help you build stronger relationships.

Building Emotional Intelligence

Remember those four attributes of emotional intelligence? They will help you build your EQ score. You will need to focus on your self-management and self-awareness first. After that, you can focus on the social awareness and relationship management piece of the puzzle. So, how do you do that?

Self-management is our ability to manage our behaviors, thoughts, and emotions in a constructive way (Munro, 2021). If you take the time to manage your emotions, it can help you react appropriately in different situations. This can be seen in today's remote workplace culture. Are you easily distracted? Are your kids running around and acting crazy? You may need to focus on staying attentive and finding ways to be productive while juggling these responsibilities. The same applies to in-person work environments.

Being self-aware is not discovering the deep dark recesses of your mind. Instead, it's about finding what makes you tick. What do you do well? What motivates you? What satisfies you? What are your pet peeves? Self-awareness helps you leverage your emotions to succeed in life and in business. Gaining self-awareness is the first step to build your emotional intelligence. "Self-awareness is a foundational skill; when you have it, self-awareness makes the other emotional intelligence skills much easier to use and the other adaptive leadership skills easier to incorporate into your repertoire" (Bradberry & Greaves, 2012, p.135).

Self-management and self-awareness go hand in hand. Successful leaders can see things for what they really are without having an emotional outburst. If you can do this consistently, you will find that the real results come from putting temporary needs on hold to pursue the bigger picture. This is the stage of the game where you will really get to know yourself. It will get uncomfortable. Lean into it. It will be worth it in the end.

Here are some self-management and self-awareness skills that can be mastered:

- Know what your responsibilities are.
- Know how you fit into your work hierarchy.
- Know how to be independent.
- Know what the goal is.

- Understand the bigger picture.
- Learn how to become a strategic planner.
- Set priorities and boundaries.
- Control your emotions.
- Practice self-care.
- Keep your promises.
- Know when to engage.
- Focus on what you can control.
- Be a team player.
- Know your limitations.
- Take breaks to recharge.
- Practice mindfulness.
- Try not to multitask too much.
- Reframe how you view self-management.
- Know your emotional triggers.
- Celebrate the positive emotions of yourself and others.

It's equally important that you begin to build your social awareness. "Social awareness is your ability to accurately pick up on emotions in other people and understand what is really going on with them. This often means perceiving what other people are thinking and feeling even if you do not feel the same way" (p. 157). Pay attention to nonverbal cues when people are speaking to you. What do those cues tell you about how they're really feeling about the situation? Remain empathetic towards others. This will help you figure out what type of power dynamics are in play and how others are feeling.

This is why being mindful was listed as a skill to master. Be present when people are speaking. You wouldn't like it if you were speaking to someone and they looked uninterested. You might be able to multitask, but it sends a negative response to the person trying to talk to you. Watch your own body language as well. Nonverbal messages can speak louder than the expressed language in any given conversation.

How to Use Your Emotional Intelligence

Emotional intelligence is a part of your everyday life. But it doesn't mean you don't need to practice from time to time. Once you master these skills, it will help you build better relationships, strengthening your emotional intelligence and your overall physical and mental health. Cherry (2020) provides a comprehensive list of ways to do this:

- Accept criticism and take responsibility.
- Be able to move on when you make a mistake.
- Say no.
- Feel free to share your feelings with other people.
- Solve problems with others' best interests in mind.
- Have and show empathy for others.
- Practice active listening.
- Be aware of why you do the things you do.
- Try not to be judgmental.

Improving Your Emotional Intelligence

How can you improve your social and emotional skills? It sounds so vague and ambiguous, but it doesn't have to be that way. There are small habits that you can master to improve your emotional intelligence. Remember that it takes 30 days to build a habit. Take your time with this and do not bite off more than you can chew.

The first thing you'll want to do is practice the active listening skills previously mentioned. You need to pay attention: full attention. Listen to the verbal and non-verbal cues in a conversation. Body language can convey so much meaning. Paraphrase and ask questions to make sure you're understanding the other person correctly.

Showing empathy is another great way to improve your emotional intelligence. This is a hard one because if you lack empathy, it can be difficult to master. It's one thing to recognize others' emotions, but it's a totally different thing to feel their situation. Put yourself in their shoes. How would you feel? Being empathetic is another interpersonal skill that will help you build stronger relationships long-term.

As we discussed, the ability to reason with emotions is a crucial part of your emotional intelligence development. How many times did your own emotions influence a decision you made or impact your behaviors? When people respond to you, try to recognize the emotions that are at play. This goes back to the empathy part. Why does that person feel that way? What is happening to cause those feelings? Take some time to reflect on the situation fully before reacting.

Here are some simple ways to move towards improving your emotional intelligence if what was discussed seems too daunting at the moment:

- Recognize and name your emotions.

- Ask others for constructive feedback.
- Study the current literature on emotional intelligence and empathy.

Potential Pitfalls

If you have a lower emotional intelligence, you will experience some struggles. It would be wise to figure out what your emotional intelligence is in the beginning of your leadership journey to avoid any unnecessary issues. "People who have fewer emotional skills tend to get into more arguments, have lower quality relationships, and have poor emotional coping skills" (Cherry, 2020).

The reverse can be a pitfall as well. People who have a higher level of emotional intelligence can cause problems too. Research suggests that people with high emotional intelligence can be less creative and innovative, have difficulty delivering negative feedback, and be manipulative or deceptive (Cherry, 2020).

Research suggests that emotional intelligence is more beneficial for followers than leaders. Emotional intelligence ends up making people incredibly good at following procedures and rules. It can also help with team building. Be careful though, it can also make you way too aware of others' feelings. If you start to avoid doing something or having tough conversations because you don't want to hurt someone's feelings, take a step back and evaluate. The job still needs to be done and sometimes hard conversations need to be had.

Don't become passive about expressing your own emotional needs. This happens when you're ultra-aware.

Make sure you do not become a doormat for others to walk all over. There is a sweet spot in between that you'll need to find. You'll need to figure out a way to navigate difficult emotions in a healthy way. You are no good to people if you're on the verge of burnout. Becoming overwhelmed and suppressing these feelings will not help anyone.

A major pitfall is that you may feel like you have a very high sense of self-awareness. "A study by Tasha Eurich found that 95 percent of participants gave themselves a high marker in self-awareness. However, using more empirical measures of self-awareness, the study found that only 10–15 percent of the cohort was truly self-aware" (Harvard Professional Development, 2019). To top that off, the most unaware individuals were managers.

Reflection Time

1. Prior to this chapter, were you aware of emotional intelligence?
2. What emotional intelligence skills will you focus on in the next 30 days?
3. Are others in your organization using emotional intelligence skills?
4. What challenges might you have regarding emotional intelligence?

Let's spend some more time doing an emotional intelligence exercise.

Think back to a time when something happened that you didn't expect. Who was there? What happened? How did you feel? What emotions can you recall? What did you remember first when recalling the situation? Did you notice any physical reactions? What was the first emotion that came to mind? How did you know it was that emotion? What were the signals? What triggered this response?

Now that we've done some reflection, it's time to take what we've learned into the field. Walk around your organization for at least fifteen minutes. Pay attention to those who work with or for you. What's going on in the office? Take a short tour daily in order to get to know people and what makes them tick. Watch for signs of emotional reactions. Look at how people keep their workspaces. What time do people become transitional in space? Does this interrupt people around them? Which people never move from their desks? Does this impact their mood? This small habit will help you gain the perspective of those who work with or for you.

8

INFLUENTIAL LEADERS OF THE WORLD

The only way on Earth to influence other people is to talk about what they want and show them how to get it. –Dale Carnegie

*A*s we wrap up our 30-day leadership journey, we should look at some examples of influential leaders around the world. Successful leaders are incredibly effective influencers. To influence people, you need to be able to motivate and energize a group of people in a shared vision and present yourself as a role model for others. The influential leaders presented in this chapter can serve as a guide to your current leadership practice. You don't have to be just like them, but try to embody some of their characteristics. There are six key traits that successful influential leaders possess: intelligence, confidence, charisma, determination, sociability, and integrity. This list is just a small sample of successful leaders.

Bill Gates

William (Bill) H. Gates III is the cofounder and chair of Microsoft Corporation. Microsoft Corporation is the world's largest developer of software for personal computers. Due to his company's success, Bill Gates was the wealthiest man in the world with an estimated $129 billion in assets as of 2022. He continues to be listed in the Forbes list of the world's wealthiest people since 1987 (Wikipedia Contributors, 2019b). Gates was fascinated, even at a young age, by computers. At the tender age of 13, he and a friend developed the first computer software program.

Gates went on to attend Harvard University but never graduated. He left college to focus on software development. In 1975, he co-founded Microsoft. Under his leadership, Microsoft quickly became a household name. They developed the Disk Operating System (MS-DOS), Windows operating system, and Internet Explorer browser. The company continues to be one of the fastest growing and most profitable companies in the world.

Given his talented leadership skills, Gates and his ex-wife established the Bill and Melinda Gates Foundation in 2000. They created this foundation in the hopes of reducing inequities and improving lives around the world. The foundation does a lot of work regarding promoting education, addressing global health issues, sponsoring libraries, and supporting housing efforts in the Pacific Northwest.

Gates began transitioning out of the day-to-day operations at Microsoft in 2006. By 2008, he fully left the day-to-day operations to pursue other business and philanthropic interests. He went on to found several other companies like

TerraPower. He has even teamed up with other influential leaders like Warren Buffett. Gates and Buffett worked together to found The Giving Pledge. This pledge was established in 2010 and other billionaires around the world have joined them to give at least half of their wealth to philanthropy.

Originally, Gates' management style was less than desirable. He gained a reputation for being distant from others and was known to have shouting matches. It was difficult to get a hold of him if you needed something. In the early 80s, Gates even conspired against his business partner who was receiving treatments for cancer at the time. He tried to reduce Paul Allen's share in Microsoft by issuing himself stock options. He was also known to bully Microsoft employees.

This drive and aggression paid off eventually but did have some drawbacks. He was goal- and task-oriented and worked tirelessly to promote the product. This type of behavior eventually came back to bite him. Microsoft was accused by the United States government of antitrust violations. Gates had to appear before congressional hearings. He adamantly defended his company, claiming that what appeared to be a "win at all costs" attitude was merely him bringing people together to make new products and to make the old ones better.

While some consider Gates to be a visionary, he's intelligent. He's also simple and straightforward. Some even claim he's unpretentious and altruistic in his later years. After stepping down from Microsoft in 2014, he has shifted his focus to philanthropy. He's demonstrated that he has a strong concern for those in poverty and those who are largely underserved in the world. He's even channeled that leadership during the pandemic to establish the COVID-19 Therapeutics Accelerator in 2020. This helped to develop and evaluate new and repurposed drugs and biologics to treat patients for COVID-19.

He's also no stranger to the climate change conversation. Gates has encouraged other leaders worldwide to take part in conversations regarding climate change and global access to energy. His mission is to make governments and private sectors invest in clean, reliable energy sources to make it environmentally not only safe but also affordable for all. In 2015, Gates led the charge for two initiatives at the United Nations Climate Change Conference in Paris.

Jack Welsh

John F. Welch Jr., or Jack for short, is another influential leader and successful American business executive. Welch was also a chemical engineer by trade and a writer. He served as the Chairman and CEO of General Electric (GE) from 1981 to 2001. When Welch retired from GE, he received the largest payment anyone in business had ever received in severance package to the tune of $417 million. By 2006, his net worth had skyrocketed to $720 million (Wikipedia Contributors, 2019c).

Welch studied chemical engineering at the University of Massachusetts Amherst. During his college years, he worked for Sunoco and PPG Industries. He had several job offers after graduation but ultimately decided to attend graduate school at the University of Illinois at Urbana-Champaign. In 1960, Welch graduated with a master's and a

PhD in chemical engineering. It was then that he joined the ranks of GE.

Welch began his career with GE as a junior chemical engineer in Massachusetts on a salary of $10,500 a year. Oddly enough, that salary today would be the equivalent of $90,000. In 1961, Welch wanted to quit because he was upset with the raise he had been given and the bureaucracy that he was experiencing at GE. The current executive convinced him to stay on and help create the culture Welsh wished to see. Even Welsh experienced some moments of crisis during his tenure at GE that almost got him fired. For example, in 1963, there was an explosion that blew the roof off the facilities that he managed.

Five years later in 1968, Welch became the vice president and head of the plastics division at GE. He quickly moved on to become the vice president of GE's metallurgical and chemical divisions in 1971. From 1973–1979, he was the head of strategic planning for GE. These positions were great exposure for the leadership roles he would hold later. During this time, he was also named senior vice president and head of the consumer products and services division. In 1979, Welch became the vice chairman of GE. Rising quickly through the ranks allowed Welch to become GE's youngest chairman and CEO in 1981. Once he became the vice chairman, he began dismantling much of what his predecessor had established.

Welch was able to increase the market value of GE from $12 billion in 1981 to $410 billion when he retired (Wikipedia Contributors, 2019c). During his tenure as chairman, Welch was able to create a work environment that embodied a small business experience at a large corporation. He wanted to have a workplace that embraced informality. The nine-layer management hierarchy was quickly destroyed under Welch's leadership. Welch also cut many parts of GE that were inefficient, closing factories, reducing payrolls, and cutting units that weren't producing.

Welch's leadership coined the term that has been popularized called the "rank and yank" policy. He would fire the bottom 10% of his managers—regardless of performance—every year. He would also reward those who were in the top 20% with bonuses and employee stock options. Eventually, he allowed the stock options to be available to almost one-third of all employees instead of the elite top execs.

Welch was no stranger to success. During his tenure, GE acquired Radio Corporation of America (RCA). Welch ended up selling off most of RCA's portfolio but kept NBC. In the 90s, he also managed to shift GE's focus from manufacturing to financial services which was done through a variety of acquisitions. He was named the Manager of the Century by Fortune magazine in 1999.

Welch was always concerned about his future successor, so he devised a succession plan and employee development into the organization. Welch was adamant about making people the core of GE. He was very aware that his departure would have a significant impact on the organization and its future. It's estimated that Welch's severance package was valued at $420 million (Wikipedia Contributors, 2019c).

Welch did not stop leading after he stepped down from GE. He became an advisor to the private equity firm Clayton, Dubilier, & Rice and to the chief executive of IAC. He went on to run the public speaking circuit and co-wrote a column in BusinessWeek with his wife, which was syndicated by The

New York Times. The book he wrote in 2005, Winning, reached number one on The Wall Street Journal bestseller list and was on the New York Times bestseller list. Just a year later, the College of Business at Sacred Heart University became known as the "John F. Welch College of Business." In 2016, the university began calling it the "Jack Welch College of Business." Welch even began teaching at the collegiate level at MIT Sloan. This course was created for a select cohort of 30 MBA students who exemplified leadership qualities.

As if all of that didn't keep him busy, Welch founded the Jack Welch Management Institute in 2009. This is a program at Chancellor University (acquired by Strayer University in 2011) that offers an online Master of Business Administration. His program was named the number one most influential education brand on LinkedIn and a top business school in 2016. The Princeton Review named it one of the Top 25 Online MBA Programs for four years running (2017-2020).

Welch passed away at his home in New York City from kidney failure at the age of 84, on March 1, 2020. He leaves behind a legacy as the most celebrated American boss. His approach to breaking down silos in the workplace continues to work today. Unfortunately, in 2021, GE broke into three public companies—aviation, health care, and energy—and has ceased to exist as it once did under Welch's leadership.

Steve Jobs

Steve Jobs was one of the most innovative minds in the business world. "He was the co-founder, chairman, and CEO of Apple; the chairman and majority shareholder of Pixar; a member of The Walt Disney Company's board of directors following its acquisition of Pixar; and the founder, chairman, and CEO of NeXT" (Wikipedia Contributors, 2018). It's amazing to think that all this success started in a garage in California.

Over his childhood and well into his college years, Jobs struggled with the traditional classroom. He was known as a troublemaker. His parents never blamed him but instead blamed the school for not challenging their brilliant son. Jobs even threatened to drop out of school at one point in middle school due to bullying. His family finally landed in the Mountain View area, which is the historic site where Apple was manifested. In 1972, Jobs started to attend Reed College, but it didn't last long. He dropped out a semester later because he claimed he didn't want to spend his parents money that they could not afford on an education that was meaningless to him.

In 1974, Jobs returned home to Los Altos and was hired by Atari, Inc. as a technician. Those who worked with Jobs found him to be difficult to deal with but a valuable resource. "He was often the smart person in the room, and he would let people know that," claimed Nolan Bushnell, Atari's co-founder (Wikipedia Contributors, 2018). During a brief time at Atari, Jobs took a spiritual trip to India as he was practicing Zen Buddhism. He returned after spending seven months in India and stayed at a commune in Oregon with some friends. He later returned to Atari in 1975. There, he created a circuit board for the arcade video game Breakout.

His business partner, Steve Wozniak, completed the first Apple I computer in 1976. Jobs suggested that they sell it.

Later that year, they founded Apple Computer Company with Ronald Wayne in the garage of Jobs' parents' home on Crist Drive. The name Apple was inspired from the commune they lived on and their lush apple orchards. Wayne left the venture for other pursuits. The infamous duo, Jobs and Wozniak, started selling personal property to order circuit boards to assemble the first Apple I computers. They sold roughly 200 units (Wikipedia Contributors, 2018). These computers consisted of a circuit board with a chip, a DuMont TV set, a Panasonic cassette tape deck, and a keyboard. Many people dismissed Jobs and his innovation.

The duo finally found success after they received funding from Mike Markkula, Intel product marketing manager and engineer. While they appreciated the funding, Jobs was not happy that Markkula had recruited Mike Scott to become the first president and CEO of Apple in 1977. Later that year, they introduced the Apple II, which was the first consumer product to be sold by Apple Computer. In 1978, Jobs' net worth climbed to over $1 million when he was only 23 years old. By the time he was 25, it jumped to $250 million (Wikipedia Contributors, 2018). Forbes named him one of the youngest people to make their list of the nation's richest people—and one of the few to do it from the ground up without inherited wealth.

In 1981, Jobs began developing Macintosh. In 1983, Jobs managed to bring on John Sculley to be Apple's CEO. However, their visions for the company were radically different from one another. Sculley ended up having little control over Jobs and the Macintosh division. This division made Apple operate like it was two separate companies which ultimately caused many people to leave, including Wozniak.

Sculley would later reorganize Apple and place Jobs in charge of New Product Development. This would ultimately take the power away from Jobs within Apple. It didn't take long for Jobs to devise a plan to get rid of Sculley. This plan was leaked, and Jobs tried to resign. The board would not accept his resignation. However, in 1985, Jobs submitted a letter of resignation and took five senior Apple employees with him to develop his next venture, NeXT.

Jobs spent the next decade working on NeXT workstations and created The Graphics Group, which was later named Pixar. Pixar partnered with Disney in 1995 to produce their first film, Toy Story. Under Jobs' leadership, the company went on to produce box-office hits such as A Bug's Life, Toy Story 2, Monsters Inc., Finding Nemo, The Incredibles, Cars, Ratatouille, WALL-E, Up, Toy Story 3, and Cars 2.

In 1996, Apple purchased NeXT for $427 million (Wikipedia Contributors, 2018). This led Jobs back to the company he co-founded. He was named the interim chief executive when then-CEO Gil Amelio was terminated in 1997. Jobs started to cut divisions that he deemed useless, leaving people fearing for their jobs. Jobs became the permanent CEO in 2000. At that point, Apple started branching out with the creation of the iPod and iTunes Store. In 2007, Apple then added the iPhone to their portfolio. It wasn't until then that Jobs embraced the attitude that open-ended innovation needed to be nurtured within his company.

Jobs also tried to take criticisms of his company to heart. In 2005, people started to complain that his company was creating too much environmental waste. He responded to this criticism by announcing that Apple would take back iPods for free at retail stores to be recycled—this was later expanded to include Macs as well.

Even though Jobs was perceived as a demanding individual who wanted perfection, he aspired to push his products to the forefront of the tech industry. He was an innovator and wanted to be the leader in style trends. He remained at the helm of Apple until his cancer diagnosis. In 2008, Bloomberg mistakenly published a 2,500-word obituary of Jobs. Not anticipating that his health concerns would become an issue, Jobs was forced to take a six-month leave of absence in 2009. During this time, Jobs received a liver transplant, where his prognosis was deemed to be excellent. In 2011, he returned to work but immediately took another medical leave of absence. He later announced in August of 2011 that he would be resigning as Apple's CEO. Shortly thereafter, Jobs passed away at his home in October 2011 from complications of a relapse of his previously treated tumor.

Warren Buffett

Warren Buffett is one of the most successful investors in the world. He was an American business magnate, investor, and philanthropist who gained his success as the chairman and CEO of Berkshire Hathaway. As of March 2022, he was the sixth-wealthiest person in the world with a net worth of over $117 billion (Wikipedia Contributors, 2019a). Growing up in the Midwest, he gained an appreciation for business and investing. It's been said that his favorite book growing up was One Thousand Ways to Make $1000. Even as a kid, he was always trying to find a way to sell something. He went door-to-door selling gum, magazines, and Coca-Cola bottles. He even ran his own paper route in 1944.

In 1947, he attended the Wharton School at the University of Pennsylvania. He later transferred back home to attend the University of Nebraska, where he graduated with a Bachelor of Science in Business Administration. Unfortunately, he was rejected by Harvard Business School. So, Buffett went on to graduate from Columbia Business School because Benjamin Graham was teaching there at the time. He graduated with a Master of Science in Economics in 1951 from Columbia. Buffett continued his education at New York Institute of Finance, where his primary focus was economics.

After graduation, he formed what was called the Buffett Partnership, Ltd. in 1956 which eventually took on Berkshire Hathaway, a textile manufacturing firm. As his investments grew and he began liquidating assets, he lived off a modest $50,000 per year and his investment income. His portfolio began to acquire stock in the Washington Post Company. His firm also acquired stock in Wesco Financial, the Buffalo Evening News, ABC, and The Coca-Cola Company. Buffett's stock is the equivalent of 7% of the company worth $1.02 billion which he still holds Wikipedia Contributors, 2019a).

To date, his annual salary was roughly $100,000. In 2008, his compensation reached $175,000 per year with a base of $100,000 (Wikipedia Contributors, 2019a). He continued to live a modest life in Omaha, Nebraska. If you're local to the area, you're likely to see him at football games at the University of Nebraska. Another fun fact about Buffett is that he never carried a cell phone or had a computer at his desk. In

2013, he apparently still owned an old Nokia flip phone and had only sent one email in his entire life. In 2020, he admitted that he finally upgraded his phone to an iPhone 11. However, he's not one to pass up luxury, either. He owns a $4 million dollar home in California and a private jet.

Buffett has suffered some setbacks during his time as a leader and investment mogul. He had to weather the storms of the mortgage crisis of 2007–2008. During that time, Berkshire Hathaway suffered a 77% loss in earnings due to the market. The estimated loss equals $25 billion during that time. He was able to navigate the crisis and ended up becoming the richest person in the world in 2008, overtaking Bill Gates' golden spot at the top.

Despite having wealth, Buffett became a philanthropist. He pledged to give away 99% of his fortune to philanthropic causes. Remember the Bill & Melinda Gates Foundation? This is how he gives away his wealth. He founded The Giving Pledge in 2009 with Bill Gates. In 2009, Buffett was elected to the American Philosophical Society. As a leader, Buffett is known for being a communicator. He's an amazing storyteller, a talent that can be seen in his annual letters to his shareholders. In 2021, he even commented on the economic impact that the COVID-19 pandemic would have on economic inequality.

He's also been known to pledge millions to a variety of initiatives in Washington that include the Nuclear Threat Initiative. He spent many years auctioning off his belongings for charity as well. Buffett continues to support his family's individual foundations as well with contributions. He's also one of the most written about men in business. "In October 2008, USA Today reported at least 47 books were in print with Buffett's name in the title" (Wikipedia Contributors, "Warren Buffett").

Reflection Time

1. What leader do you find to be inspirational or influential?
2. What traits do they possess?
3. Do you possess those traits?
4. If not, how can you develop those traits?

Leave a 1-Click Review!

I would be incredibly thankful if you could take just 60 seconds to write a brief review on Amazon, even if it's just a few sentences!

Click here to leave a quick review!

CONCLUSION

Leadership is not about titles, positions or flowcharts. It is about one life influencing another. –John C. Maxwell

Congratulations! You've embarked on a remarkable journey in the world of leadership. You have now reached the end of the book and while you might not think that's noteworthy, it is. You stuck with it and your willingness to apply this knowledge in your life is worth celebrating. It takes grit to take a step in the right direction to have success in your personal life and in the workplace.

You may have found that many items in this book were common sense. Ironically enough, the mundane is usually overlooked and is critical to lead you to the bigger picture. Taking the time to build small habits over time will help you grow and see the fruits of your labor.

Even though you've made it to the end of your 30-day leadership journey, there's still more of the game to be played. Now is the time to start keeping a record of your playbook so you can continue to win. What kind of strategies will you implement? What is your next step? Always be looking toward the future.

Learning is Never Out for the Pro

Ever hear the saying "leaders are readers"? "According to a 2007 Associated Press Poll conducted by IPSOS Public Affairs, 27 percent (one of every four) of the general population of Americans surveyed admitted to not having read even one book over the course of the prior year" (Van Hooser, 2013, p. 259). Make the commitment now to become a reader if you aren't already. Find books that will help you with personal or professional challenges that you could encounter in the future.

Learning requires a significant commitment for anyone. It will make you stretch in ways that you may not expect. You might have to let go of past experiences or think from a different perspective. When looking for new learning opportunities, take the time to broaden your horizons. Choose a book or course that will make you uncomfortable in a good way. It will help you gain new skills and become more effective as a leader.

If you're not willing to learn, you will not grow. Don't let your ego get the best of you. There is always more to learn. Just because you've made it to the top of the workplace food chain doesn't mean you know everything. Be humble. You'll become more human to those who work with and for you if you recognize that there are different ways of doing things than just accepting the status quo. Read a book, take a course, and do something.

You may even want to consider learning from consultants in your field. These individuals don't have much skin in the game since they're hired on for a short time and then go away. Due to this, they can give you honest feedback of what they see within your organization and how your employees perceive the workplace. They may have suggestions for you to implement that could impact your overall vision for the future as a leader.

The same can be said about your personal network. You'll only want to share with trusted individuals. They have a different perspective to help you gain some insight on whatever leadership challenges you might be experiencing. Of course, act with integrity and don't provide them with sensitive information.

Lead by Example

Be committed to leading by example. Be a leader that others want to emulate. To accomplish this, you need to dedicate the time to mastering your leadership skills. You don't have to be the most educated person nor the most outgoing to be successful as a leader. You must be consistent.

One way to do this is to keep track of what you're working on for professional development. Do you journal? If you don't, now is the time to get the pen and paper ready. Keep a personal leadership journey. Write down anything that comes to mind during your journey. This could be ideas, strategies, quotes, books… anything that helps you or motivates you.

Create one to three achievable goals that you want to accomplish in the next 30–90 days. What strategies will you

Conclusion

need to implement to achieve those goals? Keep track of your progress in your journal. Take note of what worked and what didn't work. What would you do differently? Choose someone you trust to share these goals with. It will help keep you accountable.

If you're serious about being a leader in your organization, share what you know with others. Keeping all this knowledge to yourself will not help your organization grow. Take the time to mentor others. Leaders develop leaders. You may even want to share this book with someone you believe could grow into greatness as a leader. Be the leader who wants to change and grow. Reinvent yourself. Inclusive leaders embrace new ideas and people in a way that makes their organizations more sustainable over time.

Now that you have all the tools, go out there and use them. Remember that this is a journey, not a race. Be gentle on yourself and others. It takes 30 days to build a habit. There will be moments where you need to pause and reassess the situation. Hopefully, some of the information presented in this text was helpful to you and your newfound journey on the path to leadership. Just by picking up this book and making it to the end is a huge accomplishment you should be proud of.

Be sure to leave a review on Amazon if you enjoyed this book. I encourage you to share your opinions, both favorable and unfavorable. Receiving constructive feedback is the only way to grow, right? This also helps other readers determine if a text is helpful. And, without this helpful feedback, I will not grow as a writer and leader. I have to be willing to walk the walk if I am willing to talk the talk.

Good luck on your leadership journey. It could be chal-

Conclusion

lenging from time to time, but now you have all the plays in your playbook for success. I do hope that you find your journey to be rewarding. And, you never know, we might be reading your name in a book one day as an influential leader. I cannot wait to read all about your successes. Today, you're one step closer to creating the future you've dreamed of.

The more intentional you are about your leadership growth, the greater your potential for becoming the leader you're capable of being. Never stop learning. –John C. Maxwell

GIFT

Just For You!

A FREE GIFT TO OUR READERS

A – Z of leadership which contain popular leadership quotes by influential leaders! Visit this link below or scan QR Code:

https://oainc.activehosted.com/f/5

REFERENCES

8 Skills All Leadership Trainings Should Teach Managers. (2019, July 19). Science of People. https://www.scienceofpeople.com/ leadership-training/#:~:text=the%20big%20question%3A-

A Single Transformational Question - Leadership Freak. (2016, October 25). Leadershipfreak.blog. https://leadershipfreak.blog/2016/10/25/a-single-transformational-question/

Allen, G., & Aweh, B. (2021, September 2). *Inside DoorDash's Leadership Accelerator for Women of Color.* Harvard Business Review. https://hbr.org/2021/09/inside-doordashs-leadership-accelerator-for-women-of-color

AZ Quotes. (n.d.). Zig Ziglar Quotes About Integrity. A-Z Quotes. Retrieved April 5, 2022, from https://www.azquotes.com/author /16182-Zig_Ziglar/tag/integrity

Becker, B. (2020). *The 7 Most Common Leadership Styles & How to Find Your Own.* Hubspot.com. https://blog.hubspot.com/ marketing/leadership-styles

Birch, A. (2022). *Top 10 Effective Leadership Principles: Defi-*

References

nition and Examples. Wikijob.co.uk.https://www.wikijob.co.uk/jobs-and-careers/employment/leadership- principles

Bradberry, T., & Graves, J. (2012). *Leadership 2.0 : [learn the secrets of adaptive leadership]*. Talentsmart, Cop.

Brown, E. (2019, October 28). *The 3 Main Types of Management Styles: A Pros and Cons List*. Unito. https://unito.io/blog/types -of-management-styles/

Callejas, R. (2016, July 7). *Which Leadership Style Are You? 3 Common Leadership Styles and What You Can Learn from Them - Salesforce Blog*. The 360 Blog from Salesforce. https://www.salesforce.com /blog/3-common-leadership-styles/

Chand, S. (2012, July 7). *4 Different Types of Leadership Styles*. Your Article Library. https://www.yourarticlelibrary.com/business-management/4-different-types-of-leadership-styles/2550

Cherry, K. (2019). *How to Become a Stronger and More Effective Leader*. Verywell Mind. https://www.verywellmind.com/ways-to-become -a-better-leader-2795324

Cherry, K. (2020, June 3). *Overview of Emotional Intelligence*. Verywell Mind. https://www.verywellmind.com/what-is-emotional- intelligence-2795423

Cockell, A. (2022, March 4). *Management Styles for Effective Leadership: Overview and Examples*. Www.wikijob.co.uk. https://www.wiki job.co.uk/content/jobs-and-careers/leadership/management-styles-for-effective-leadership

Corsey, M. (2021, July 12). *Leadership Training Can Pay Huge Dividends for Midsize Companies*. Harvard Business Review. https://hbr.org/2021/07/leadership-training-can-pay-huge-dividends-for-midsize-companies

Daum, K. (2016, May 31). 29 Great Leadership Quotes

References

From John F. Kennedy. Inc.com. https://www.inc.com/kevin-daum/29-great-leadership-quotes-from-john-fitzgerald-kennedy.html

Doyle, A. (2013, August 20). *Top 10 Leadership Skills Employers Look For*. The Balance Careers; The Balance. https://www.thebalancecareers.com/top-leadership-skills-2063782

Eastwood, B. (2019, January 24). *The 5 Qualities All Successful Leaders Have in Common*. Northeastern University Graduate Programs. https://www.northeastern.edu/graduate/blog/top-5-leadership-qualities/

Financhill. (2020, July 14). *Elon Musk Leadership Style*. Financhill. https://financhill.com/blog/investing/elon-musk-leadership-style

Fisher, R., Ury, W., & Patton, B. (1991). *Getting to yes : negotiating agreement without giving in*. Penguin.

Graduate Programs Staff. (2019, September 4). *5 Essential Leadership Skills for the Workplace of Tomorrow*. Northeastern University Graduate Programs. https://www.northeastern.edu/graduate/blog/essential-leadership-skills-for-tomorrow/

Greenleaf Center for Servant Leadership. (2016). *What is servant leadership?* Greenleaf Center for Servant Leadership. https://www.greenleaf.org/what-is-servant-leadership/

Gundling, E., & Williams, C. (2021). *Inclusive Leadership: Global Impact*. Aperian Global.

Harvard Professional Development. (2019, August 26). *How to Improve Your Emotional Intelligence*. Professional Development | Harvard DCE. https://professional.dce.harvard.edu/blog/how-to-improve-your-emotional-intelligence/#content

References

Hayes, A. (2021, June 27). *Macro Manager*. Investopedia. https://www.investopedia.com/ terms/m/macro-manager.asp

http://facebook.com/careersidekick. (2017, September 5). *10 Leadership Experience Examples for Interviews and Resumes - Career Sidekick*. Career Sidekick. https://careersidekick.com/what-are-your- leadership-experiences/

https://www.facebook.com/thebalancecom. (2018). *Visionary Leadership Has 3 Characteristics You Want to Find and Follow*. The Balance Careers. https://www.thebalancecareers.com /visionary-leadership -4174279

Iannacci, N. (2016, April 12). *Henry Clay, the great compromiser - National Constitution Center*. National Constitution Center – Constitutioncenter.org. https://constitution center.org/blog/ henry-clay-the-great-compromiser

Institute for Health and Human Potential. (2019). *What Is Emotional Intelligence, Daniel Goleman*. IHHP. https://www.i-hhp.com/ meaning-of-emotional-intelligence/

Kagan, J. (2020, February 4). *Micromanager*. Investopedia. https://www.investopedia.com/terms /m/micro-manager.asp

Kasprzak, L. (2018, December 14). *Leading a Diverse Team*. www.aiche.org. https://www.aiche .org/chenected/2018/12/leading -diverse-team

Kouzes, J. M., & Posner, B. Z. (2012). *The Leadership Challenge : How to Make Extraordinary Things Happen in Organizations Ed. 5*. Jossey Bass Inc.

Kruse, K. (2013, April 9). *What Is Leadership?* Forbes. https://www.forbes.com/sites/ kevinkruse/2013/04/09/what-is-leadership/?sh=1a3a99e75b90

Kurt, S. (2021, March 31). *Herzberg's motivation-hygiene theory: Two-factor*. Education Library. https://educationlibrary.org/ herzbergs-motivation-hygiene-theory-two-factor/

References

Lebow, H. (2021, June 7). *Emotional Intelligence (EQ)*. Psych Central. https://psychcentral.com/ lib/what-is-emotional-intelligence-eq#why-its-important

Lucas, S. (2016, October 25). *A Single Transformational Question - Leadership Freak*. Leadershipfreak.blog. https://leadership freak.blog/2016/10/25/a-single-transformational -question/

Mind Tools Content Team. (2009a). *Team Management Skills: The Core Skills Needed to Manage Your Team*. Mindtools.com. https://www.mindtools.com/pages/article/newTMM_92.htm

Mind Tools Content Team. (2009b). *What Is Leadership?* Mindtools.com. https://www.mindtools.com/pages/article/newLDR_41.htm

MindTools. (2009). *Transformational LeadershipBecoming an Inspirational Leader*. Mindtools.com.https://www.mindtools.com/ pages/article/transformational- leadership.htm

Moore, C. (2019, January 9). *Emotional intelligence skills and how to develop them*. PositivePsychology.com. https://positivepsychology .com/emotional-intelligence-skills/

Morgan, D. (2020, May 14). *What is McClelland's Human Motivation Theory - a blog by Business Butler*. Business Butler. https://www.businessbutleruk.com/blog/management/ mcclellands-human-motivation-theory

Morgan, J. (2020, January 6). *What is leadership, and who is a leader?* Chief Learning Officer - CLO Media. https://www.chieflearning officer.com/2020/01/06/what-is-leadership-and-
who-is-a-leader/

Munro, I. (2021, February 15). *What Is self-management, and how can you improve it? | BetterUp*.https://www.betterup.-

com/blog/what-is-self-management-and-how-can-you-improve-it

Path-Goal Theory of Leadership. (2013). Nwlink.com. http://www.nwlink.com/~donclark/leader/lead_path_goal.html

Peter Guy Northouse. (2021). *Introduction to leadership : concepts and practice* (5th ed.). Sage.

Plummer, E. (2022, March 1). *The Top 10 Nonverbal Communications Skills You Need to Learn in 2021.* Www.wikijob.co.uk. https://www.wikijob.co.uk/content/interview-advice/competencies/nonverbal-communications-skills

Prentice, W. C. H. (2014, January). *Understanding leadership.* Harvard Business Review; Harvard Business Review. https://hbr.org/2004/01/understanding-leadership

ROBBINS, T. (2019). *What is Leadership? A Comprehensive Guide to Outstanding Leadership.* Tonyrobbins.com. https://www.tony robbins.com/what-is-leadership/

Segal, J., Smith, M., Robinson, L., & Shubin, J. (2019). *Improving Emotional Intelligence (EQ).* HelpGuide.org. https://www.helpguide.org/articles/mental-health/emotional-intelligence-eq.htm

Sherlock, C. (2021, January 19). *8 Pitfalls of Emotional Intelligence: A Summary.* LinkedIn. https://www.linkedin.com/pulse/8-pitfalls-emotional-intelligence-summary-catherine-sherlock/

Shonk, K. (2019, September 30). *Top 10 Negotiation Skills.* PON - Program on Negotiation at Harvard Law School. https://www.pon.harvard.edu/daily/negotiation-skills-daily/top-10-negotiation-skills/

Sirota's Three-Factor Theory. (2016, November 10). Free

References

Management Books. http://www.free-management-ebooks.com/news/sirotas-three-factor-theory/#:~:text=Sirota

Skillsyouneed. (2011). *What is Negotiation? - Introduction to Negotiation | SkillsYouNeed.* Skillsyouneed.com. https://www.skillsyouneed.com/ips/negotiation.html

Twin, A. (2020, July 25). *Leadership: Achieving Goals, Tackling Competition, Inspiring Employees.* Investopedia. https://www.investopedia.com/terms/l/leadership.asp

University of Washington. (2022). *In Group/Out Group lesson plan: Interrupting bias.* Center for Teaching and Learning. https://teaching.washington.edu/programs/theater-for-change/tfc-lesson-plans/in-groupout-group-lesson-plan-interrupting-bias/

Watershed Associates. (2019). *Negotiation Stages Introduction.* Watershedassociates.com. https://www.watershedassociates.com/learning-center-item/negotiation-stages-introduction.html

Western Governors University. (2020, August 10). *A Guide to Transformational Leadership.* Western Governors University. https://www.wgu.edu/blog/guide-transformational-leadership2008.html#close

WGU. (2020, October 27). *What Is Visionary Leadership?* Western Governors University. https://www.wgu.edu/blog/visionary-leadership2010.html

What is Visionary Leadership and Who is a Visionary Leader? (2022, February 23). The Black Sheep Community. https://www.theblacksheep.community/visionary-leadership/

Wikipedia Contributors. (2018, November 28). *Steve Jobs.* Wikipedia; Wikimedia Foundation. https://en.wikipedia.org/wiki/Steve_Jobs

References

Wikipedia Contributors. (2019a, March 27). *Warren Buffett*. Wikipedia; Wikimedia Foundation. https://en.wikipedia.org/wiki/Warren_Buffett

Wikipedia Contributors. (2019b, April 11). *Bill Gates*. Wikipedia; Wikimedia Foundation. https://en.wikipedia.org/wiki/Bill_Gates

Wikipedia Contributors. (2019c, May 15). *Jack Welch*. Wikipedia; Wikimedia Foundation. https://en.wikipedia.org/wiki/Jack_Welch

Wikipedia Contributors. (2019d, July 7). *Servant leadership*. Wikipedia; Wikimedia Foundation. https://en.wikipedia.org/wiki/Servant_leadership

Wikipedia Contributors. (2020, June 19). *Microaggression*. Wikipedia. https://en.wikipedia.org/wiki/Microaggression#:~:text=Microaggression%20is%20a%20term%20used

Yan, A. (2019). *How to Improve Your Leadership Skills*. Investopedia. https://www.investopedia.com/articles/pf/12/leadership-skils.asp

www.ingramcontent.com/pod-product-compliance
Lightning Source LLC
Chambersburg PA
CBHW050244120526
44590CB00016B/2205